MONU-MENTAL
ABOUT
Prehistoric Waterford

T0333570

MONU-MENTAL
ABOUT
Prehistoric Waterford

TOM FOURWINDS

NONSUCH

To the amazing women in my life – Janet, Uta, Nirvana and Lyzzi – thank you for being there for me.

First published 2007

Nonsuch Publishing
73 Lower Leeson Street
Dublin 2, Ireland
www.nonsuch-publishing.com

© Tom Fourwinds 2007

The right of Tom Fourwinds to be identified as the Author
of this work has been asserted in accordance with the
Copyrights, Designs and Patents Act 1988.

All rights reserved. No part of this book may be reprinted or
reproduced or utilised in any form or by any electronic, mechanical
or other means, now known or hereafter invented, including
photocopying and recording, or in any information storage or
retrieval system, without the permission in writing from the
Publishers.

British Library Cataloguing in Publication Data.
A catalogue record for this book is available from the British Library.

ISBN 978 1 84588 599 1

Typesetting and origination by NPI Media Group
Printed in Great Britain

Contents

Foreword

From the moment *Monu-Mental About Prehistoric Dublin* was published conversations started going like this:

'Which county are you doing next?'

'Waterford.'

'Waterford? Why Waterford? Aren't you going to do one of the big ones, like Cork or Sligo?'

'But Waterford is one of the big ones. It's just that most people don't know it yet!'

Waterford has so much to offer and, for people crossing to Rosslare by ferry on their way to see the monuments of County Cork, it is en route. Furthermore, it is only a small diversion if you are travelling from Dublin to Cork. So, with the help of this book, people making the journey will hopefully be able to take in some of Waterford's wonderful monuments.

I feel a bit sorry for the county in ways. People interested in ancient sites often drive straight through it or bypass it and head directly for Cork and Kerry. In doing so, they are missing out on so much: amazing portal tombs such as **Knockeen** and **Gaulstown**, distinctive passage tombs at **Matthewstown** and **Harristown** and the **Ballymote** standing stone, to name but a few, should be on everyone's itinerary. Obviously this short list is not all there is to see. If that were the case then there wouldn't be much point in a book like this. County Waterford has some real treasures beyond the selection of 'show sites' mentioned above.

One of my issues with County Dublin was the total lack of signposted monuments. County Waterford is very lucky, because many of the best ones (but by no means all of them) are signposted. Considering the rate at which our heritage is being destroyed, this is a luxury that people should take advantage of. The more people that frequent the sites with public access the more likely it is that the other sites will be preserved and not bulldozed in the pursuit of the Euro.

Introduction

County Waterford offers a wide variety of prehistoric monuments that includes most of the major types, but it is often overlooked in this respect due to its strong Viking connection and the wealth of monuments found in its neighbouring county, Cork. Indeed, the name Waterford possibly derives from the Viking name for the estuary – *Vader-fjord*[1] – and does not mean 'a ford over the water'. Vader or Vidar is the son of Odin and it is said that he will avenge his father's death after *Ragnarök* – the final conflict in Norse mythology. The old Irish name for Waterford – *Cuan-na-Groth* (Harbour of the Sun) – is much more poetic and may have links to ancient practices. In 1824 Revd R.H. Ryland wrote:

> … the inhabitants at the time were Pagans, worshippers of the sun, and it was in honour of their deity, that the town received its primary appellation. There is a tradition still preserved, that on days of solemn worship, the people of the town were wont to march in procession to a high conical hill, in the adjoining county of Kilkenny, where, on its elevated summit, they worshipped and offered sacrifice to their God. The place alluded to is now generally called Tory Hill, but at that time, and even at the present day, it is only known in the Irish language, as the Hill of the Sun.[2]

Another possible derivation with Norse roots could come from *Varder-fjord* – The Fjord/Estuary of the Cairns. The passage tomb at **Harristown** overlooks the entrance to the estuary and there may well have been more when the Vikings first sailed inland from the Atlantic and up the River Suir.

Today, by far the most numerous type of monument to be found in the county is the standing stone. These can reach heights of over 3 metres, with some, such as the finely shaped example at **Ballymote**, being over 4 metres tall. Scattered across the county is an excellent selection of megalithic tombs with all the main classifications being represented.

As well as the vast quantity of seemingly isolated tombs and standing stones in Waterford, there is an incredible megalithic complex on the top of the Monavullagh Mountains centred on Coumeraglin Mountain, that includes cairns,

Ballymote standing stone.

stone circles, enclosures, standing stones and a possible court tomb.[3] The first time I walked across Coumeraglin Mountain I saw monuments appearing out of the mist from every direction, and I realised the area was of major significance and needed to be investigated properly. M. Moore surveyed this complex for the *Archaeological Inventory of County Waterford* and the findings were also published in the *Proceedings of the Prehistoric Society*.[4] I was immensely pleased to find the above report and to see that it had been undertaken with such diligence and attention to detail, although I am not sure about some of its conclusions.

The Monavullagh Mountains run down the county from north to south, roughly dividing it in two, and providing me with a convenient way of splitting up the country when discussing its monuments. This natural feature is a useful dividing line to take advantage of, because all the megalithic tombs are to the east of it, while to the west standing stones prevail.

Throughout Ireland access to sites is nearly always granted once permission has been sought. The good preservation of many of the monuments indicates that the farmers of County Waterford have been very tolerant in the past of the monuments in their fields and this continues today. There is even a 'dolmen trail'– a signposted route that takes you to many of the finer tombs. However, some sites that are signed can still prove tricky to find: the portal tomb at **Knockeen**, for example, is missing its final sign telling you where to leave the road if you wish to see it.

Ogham stones are very common in Waterford, but I have not even attempted to list them all here. The ones that I have included are those that appear to be 'oghamised' standing stones. The site at **Drumlohan** is included because of its significance. Many of the others are worth seeking out though, especially the ones at Kiltera and Mount Melleray Monastery.

The group of tombs known as The Tramore Passage Tombs, along with their links to Scilly, are discussed in the first chapter (East Waterford), but I will take this opportunity to introduce one possible reason why Waterford should be considered such an important part of prehistoric Ireland. The Scilly Isles, a group of islands 45 kilometres from Land's End in Cornwall, England, has a very large concentration of megalithic tombs for their land mass. The relationship between the designs of some tombs in the Scilly Isles and Cornwall is not surprising, but the link to Waterford is somewhat more puzzling. The one thing that links them all together is bronze. Cornwall has vast reserves of tin, whilst southern Ireland is rich in copper.[5] Anyone controlling the supply of both would be in a very powerful position. The Scilly Isles is ideally placed to control trade between Ireland and Cornwall. The coast of Waterford offers many safe landing spots and the Suir estuary is an ideal waterway for travelling inland. It would be sensible for a civilisation based in the Scilly Isles to have footholds in both Cornwall and south Ireland, which would explain the presence of similar tombs in those areas.

Those not familiar with the defining characteristics of the types of monuments featured in this book may want to read the chapter 'Monument Type Descriptions' before reading the next section.

Sites mentioned in the text that appear in **bold italics** are featured in the gazetteer section.

About the Monuments
of County Waterford

East Waterford

The group of monuments known as the Tramore Group are located in the eastern part of the county. This group consists of three passage tombs at *Carriglong*, *Harristown* and *Matthewstown*, and two smaller monuments at *Carrickavrantry* and *Munmahoge*. The latter two were once classified in the same category as the three passage tombs, but a 'reconsideration' by Ó Nualláin and Walsh[6] suggested they should be classified as wedge tombs. The reasoning behind this is that the chambers of these tombs do not open onto the kerb via a passage, but are closed and were completely covered by their cairns. This does make them more akin to Irish wedge tombs than passage tombs, but another likeness was overlooked. The similarities between the Tramore passage tombs and the gallery graves of the Scilly Isles have long been commented upon,[7] but there are two other kinds of Scillonian tomb, one of which was called the 'closed chamber' by H. O'Neill Hencken.[8] He describes this type as '… *the* closed chamber, *also of large stones but having no entrance.*' These are strikingly similar to *Carrickavrantry* and *Munmahoge* and perhaps these two monuments should be grouped with these Scillonian examples, rather than with Irish wedge tombs.

The most easterly of this group is at *Harristown*. This east-facing monument is built at the southern end of a north-south-aligned rocky plateau that overlooks the estuarine entrance to Waterford harbour and also offers tremendous views to the south and west. The views to the north are obscured naturally by the top of a low hill and unnaturally by radio masts that do their utmost to ruin the peacefulness of this remarkable location.

The *Harristown* tomb consists of a 7-metre-long undifferentiated passage inside a 10-metre-diameter kerb of large stones. (An undifferentiated passage is one where there is no distinction between the passage and the chamber.) One roof-stone remains in place at the west end. If this monument did follow the same design pattern as the Scillonian examples, then a low 'bun-shaped' cairn, rather than a higher hemi-spherical cairn, would have covered the central structure, leaving the kerb exposed. In 1868 a paper by Revd George Reade referred to

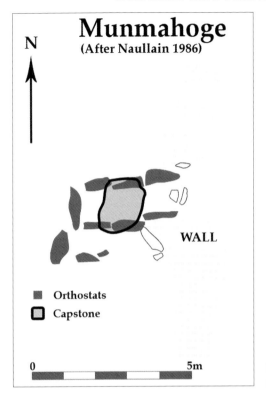

Munmahoge
(After Naullain 1986)

N

WALL

■ Orthostats
□ Capstone

0   5m

Plan of Munmahoge 'wedge' tomb,
after Ó Nualláin.

this monument as Carrick-a-Dhirra, probably a perversion of the goddess's name
that gives the Beara Peninsula and the Calliagh Birra's House (a passage tomb on
Slieve Gullion, County Armagh) their names. Wood-Martin said that the name
referred to the rocky hill on which the tomb stands.[9]

During extensive excavation work in 1939, carried out by Jacquetta
Hawkes,[10] there were only a few finds. These included the cremated remains
of probably two bodies as primary burials. An 'axe-amulet and a pebble of
similar shape' were found alongside these burials. Although treasure seekers
disturbed the ground inside the passage, it is believed that nothing significant
was taken from the tomb and that these two items were the only non-per-
ishable objects placed in the chamber during its first phase of use. Later in
the tomb's history, many secondary Bronze Age burials were placed in and
around the chamber/passage. Cinerary urns accompanied these later cremation deposits, along with a pygmy cup, a bronze blade, stone beads and bone
pins.

Before the cairn was laid over the megalithic structure, burning branches were
placed around the passage and gallery and their remains were not cleared away.
Was this a ritual purification of the site? Did this practice take place elsewhere,
but was not detected because the burnt wood was cleared away?

Above: Harristown by Reade, from Borlase's *Dolmens of Ireland*.

Right: An urn from Harristown (After Hawkes).

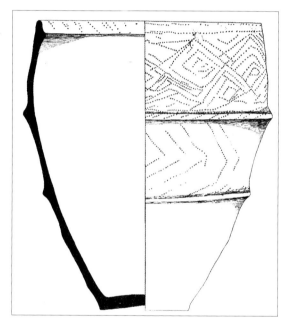

In 1824, Revd R. H. Ryland described the monument as being five stones placed side by side and surrounded by 'a circle of stones about thirty yards in diameter'. Indeed, the plan of **Harristown** in Borlase's *Dolmens of Ireland* clearly shows five roof-stones *in situ*. Ryland went on to say that, 'It is supposed to have been a seat of justice, or probably the grave of some hero',[11] but he did not elaborate on an associated folklore.

Some 6 kilometres to the north of **Harristown**, in **Ballygunnertemple** TD, there is a ruined double cist a few metres from the Waterford to Passage East road. Two parallel slabs represent one of the chambers, while two perpendicular slabs are all that remain of the other. They occupy a spot beneath a cluster of tall trees next to a long, private driveway. The undergrowth beneath the trees makes it quite difficult to tell exactly what is going on here. The site is known as Mount Druid

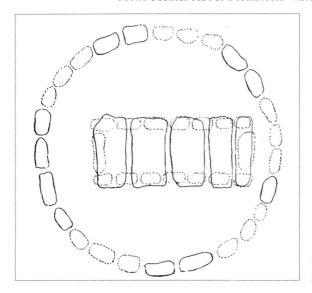

Plan of Harristown from
Borlase's *Dolmens of Ireland.*

and the early Ordnance Survey maps marked it as Druid's Altar. In *The Dolmens of Ireland*, W.C. Borlase[12] quoted from Ryland's *History of Waterford*:

> Ryland speaks of this as 'a stone pointed out as a cromlech or "Druid's Altar"', and
> in his opinion it was 'altogether too minute to deserve the appellation with which
> it has been dignified'.[13]

Five kilometres south-west of **Harristown** in **Ballymacaw** TD there is a standing stone 20 metres from the coast that overlooks the Atlantic Ocean. It is just under 2 metres tall and stands on open farmland that slopes upwards to the east. To the west there are wide sweeping bays and just 50 metres from the stone there is a small, rocky cove. The sound of the surf crashing into the rocks below creates a wonderful atmosphere. The top of the stone has been damaged, which gives it the appearance of a shouldered torso. It is known locally as The White Wife, so perhaps the stone was deliberately shaped to resemble a person.

The closest monument to Waterford city centre is the portal tomb in **Ballindud** TD. This is one of the more neglected tombs in the county and stands at the edge of a field next to a hedgerow, and is covered in brambles. The capstone is a large, nearly round stone and is held off the ground by two stones that are now collapsed. In 1824 it was in considerably better condition and the diagram used by W.C. Borlase shows the capstone supported at one end by two portal stones with the other end resting on the ground next to the backstone. In this state it looks similar to the portal tomb at **Ballyquin** and throws some light on the original form of that monument. In a field to the east of the tomb, also in **Ballindud** TD, there is a short standing stone.

In *Carriglong* TD, 3.5 kilometres south of *Ballindud*, is another of the Tramore passage tombs. Like the *Harristown* example, this was excavated in 1939, but by T.G.E. Powell.[14] The passage is marginally shorter than that of the *Harristown* monument and is aligned slightly south of east. The kerb is more complete, but the gallery is less well preserved. Treasure seekers caused the damage to the passage when they dug two pits. The archaeological finds were interesting, in that they differ from those found in the similarly designed tombs on the Scilly Isles. They included pottery sherds (some of which had been decorated), several flint scrapers and a flint beach pebble. Powell considered these to be primary deposits.[15]

A little over 1 kilometre south there is a standing stone in *Pickardstown* TD. This is over 1.5 metres tall and occupies a spot on the northern end of a low spur.

Moving north-west we find two very different megalithic tombs. The first is the wedge tomb at *Munmahoge*. Hidden away in a wide hedgerow, this site is rarely visited, but a small clearing inside the hedge does allow it to be studied with some ease. The gallery is aligned east-west. A single roof-stone remains *in situ* at the west end. The gallery walls are complete on the south side, but the north side has been damaged. Two large stones lean against the bank to the south of the monument, which are probably displaced roof-stones. The tomb stands near to the top of a steep bank that drops down to a stream to the north.

Just beyond *Munmahoge*, in *Knockeen* TD, stands one of Ireland's finest portal tombs. It is rather surprising that the monument has fared so well, as it is now incorporated into the wall of the graveyard of the old Kilburne parish church, which has long lain in ruin. The building of the church next to the tomb adds wonderfully to the longevity of this site's sacredness. There are two capstones, the upper of which stands an impressive 4 metres high. The two portal stones and the second capstone, which covers the chamber, support the upper capstone so that it is horizontal. There is a full-height doorstone and access into the chamber is only possible via a small aperture in the southern wall of the chamber or through a narrow gap between the backstone and the north side-stone. The central axis is aligned east-west with the portal unusually at the west end.

In his *Rude Stone Monuments*[16] Fergusson remarks that 'it neither has any surroundings nor any traditions attached to it', which is odd considering its proximity to the parish church. He continues by erroneously suggesting that 'it looks as if we are approaching the form out of which Stonehenge grew, which, I have not a doubt, could be found in Ireland if looked for'. The recess formed by the portal stones and doorstone is also commented upon by Fergusson: 'The cell is well formed, but in front of it is a demi-cell, or ante-chamber, which looks as if it might have been used for making offerings to the dead after the cell was closed.'

The county's other wedge tomb is 4 kilometres to the south-south-east in *Carrickavrantry* TD. This occupies the corner of a field and is incorporated into a field wall. The partially uncovered gallery is 2 metres long and 1 metre wide. It is aligned north-east to south-west and is open at the south-west. A roof slab

Knockeen
'From the
NE', taken
from Du
Noyer's 1860s
report.

remains in place over the north-east end of the gallery. The wall cuts off the
south-east section of the cairn, which is still well preserved around the rest of the
monument. A few stones protrude from the cairn, some of which may represent
a kerb.

Due north of **Carrickavrantry** is a large, but damaged, standing stone in
Ballynaclogh South TD. Even though the top of this stone appears to have been
broken off, it still reaches over 2.5 metres tall.

Two kilometres to the north, on the other side of a low, rocky hillock called
Carrick-a-Roirk Hill (the Rock of the Prospect),[17] is one of the country's finest
portal tombs. **Gaulstown** portal tomb now stands in a small clearing surrounded
by trees and bushes. The 3-metre-long capstone is held 2.5 metres above the
ground by large portal stones and the backstone. There is no doorstone. The central axis is aligned east-west with the portal facing east. Sadly, the trees around this
site do not allow you to see the front very well. A drawing from the mid-1800s[18]
shows that the tomb once stood at the edge of a field in open, rough pasture
with extensive views in the direction of the Monavullagh Mountains some 25
kilometres to the east. Thirty metres to the rear of the tomb, just inside the gate
into the enclosure, there is a large cist that was originally covered by three slabs,
one of which remains. This was presumably a later insertion into the now-missing
long cairn.

A further 2 kilometres north, beneath buzzing overhead power cables, there is
a strangely shaped standing stone in **Whitfield North** TD. The stone has a large

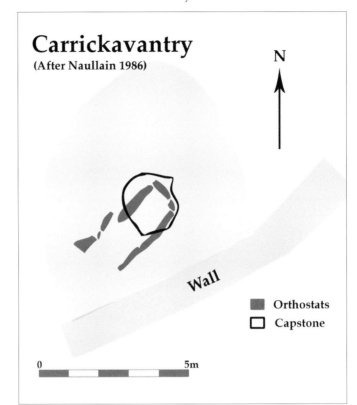

Right: Plan of Carrickavrantry, after Ó Nualláin.

Below: The kist to the rear of Gaulstown portal tomb.

Gaulstown from Du Noyer's 1860s report in the *Kilkenny Journal.*

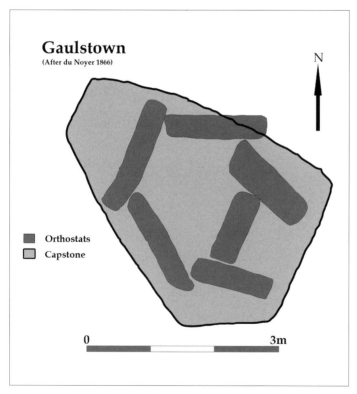

Plan of Gaulstown, after Ó Nualláin.

protuberance at the top of the east side that lends it its name – The Harp Stone. When you approach the stone, the towering pylons make it look rather small. However, this illusion is short-lived as its 3-metre height soon makes its presence known. Today, high hedgerows interrupt most of the views from this 3-metre-tall stone, but they are still open to the north-east.

It was in the Whitfield area that one of Waterford's finest monuments may have once stood. This was a passage tomb that was destroyed in the nineteenth century when its stones were removed for use as building material. Revd R H Ryland recorded this in 1824:

> On the removal of a vast heap of stones which lay for ages at the side of the road … a large flag was observed, which, when removed, discovered a large circular opening into an arched or vaulted apartment constructed in the shape of a beehive. It was composed of flat stones, the higher projecting beyond the lower, and tapered into a point which was covered with a flag. On entering into it, a narrow passage was discovered, leading from one side, but it was almost filled up with rubbish and clay: another chamber was found at no great distance. These buildings are about five or six feet high, and are supposed to have been used as tombs.[19]

Often when beehive chambers are mentioned they can be assumed to refer to souterrains, but here we have clear indication that this was, in fact, a passage tomb. Firstly, it was covered by a cairn and secondly Ryland referred to the chambers as 'buildings', implying they were above ground. From the description of the design of the monument it is obvious that it would not have been classified along with the Tramore group of passage tombs to the south, but was a more classical-styled passage tomb. With its proximity to the decorated passage tomb at Knockroe (County Kilkenny) just 25 kilometres to the north this example could have been of major archaeological significance.

Due west, in **Powersknock** TD, there is another standing stone. This is less interesting than the previous one, being rather uniform and shorter, at 'just' 2 metres. If it wasn't so close to the previous and next stones it would be remarkable, but they do overshadow this one somewhat. This stone's substantial size is masked by the ever-present nettles and other weeds that grow around its base.

Heading south again we find a beautiful standing stone in **Ballymoat** TD. This 3.7-metre-tall monster stone is a sculptural marvel. It is reminiscent of the outlying stone known as Long Meg that stands next to the Cumbrian stone circle called Long Meg and Her Daughters in England's Lake District. The stone stands above the Ballymoat Stream, which runs north into the River Suir. On the other side of the stream, to the north-east, is the rocky hill that overlooks the **Gaulstown** portal tomb. One hundred metres or so south-west of the stone, still in **Ballymoat** TD, there is a 15-metre-diameter artificial mound or cairn that is presumably a burial mound associated with the standing stone.

Long Meg (left) and Ballymoat
standing stones.

Two and a half kilometres to the south of **Ballymoat** and 2.2 kilometres west of the wedge tomb at **Carrickavrantry** is the third of the Tramore passage tombs in **Matthewstown** TD. This monument is a lot easier to appreciate than those at **Carriglong** and **Harristown** due to being situated on open grassland. The 4-metre section of the passage, which was probably twice that length originally, is completely covered by roof-stones, but the kerb is only *in situ* at the rear. It is located on a low hillock that overlooks the east end of an east-west-aligned valley. Well-manicured hedges and a weighbridge obscure views to the east.

Moving west again there is a small cluster of three monuments centred on Dunhill village, 2.5 kilometres away. The first of these is the **Dunhill** portal tomb, 500 metres south of the village in a field next to the road. This is the most ruined of Waterford's tombs, with its large, bulbous capstone resting on several collapsed stones from the chamber and some drystone walling. This is the tomb referred to by Borlase and others as being in Ballyphilip TD. A photograph that appeared in volume 2 of *Journal of the Waterford and South-East of Ireland Archaeological Society* in 1896 (p71) shows the tomb incorporated into a field wall.

One kilometre to the north of Dunhill are a pair of standing stones in **Croagh** TD. These are behind high fences around a deer farm and are inaccessible. The same distance to the east, in **Ballynageeragh** TD, there is another portal tomb. This is in considerably better condition than the **Dunhill** example, but does appear to be missing several of its structural stones. The large 3-metre-long capstone is held aloft by the doorstone and a brick/concrete support at the other end. A small sign

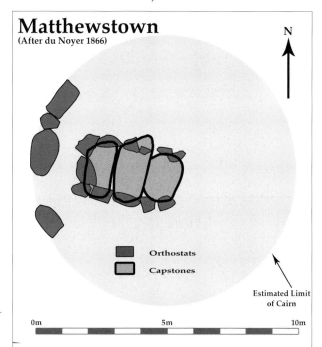

Matthewstown
(After du Noyer 1866)

N

Orthostats

Capstones

Estimated Limit
of Cairn

0m   5m   10m

Right: Plan of
Matthewstown passage
tomb.

Below: The remains of
Dunhill portal tomb,
from Borlase's *Dolmens of
Ireland*, originally from a
sketch by Du Noyer.

on the concrete wall states that P. Murray & Sons added it in 1944. The portal stones are missing, but the wall slabs from the chamber are present. Mongey postulated that the portal stones never existed, making it a hybrid portal tomb/kist:

> … the position of the 'septal', the absence of scratching on the capstone … seem to rule out the possibility of a portal having once existed. The absence of the Portal must be taken as the result of a deliberate act of the tomb-builders; and *typologically*, the tomb must be regarded as the link between the Portal Dolmen and the simple, oblong four-slabbed tombs so common in parts of the country.[20]

Near to the south coast, just east of Annestown, in Woodstown TD, there used to be two standing stones. One of these overlooked Annestown beach and Dunabrattin Bay. The other was 500 metres inland. The coastal stone has disappeared, either as a result of land clearance by the farmer or due to coastal erosion, which is quite extreme in this area. The stone may have marked the relatively easy landing place that the beach offers.

At *Savagetown*, 3 kilometres to the west of Dunhill village, there is another portal tomb. A short standing stone to the north was removed as recently as the 1980s.[21] The state of the portal tomb is hard to assess as it is now built into a thick field ditch*that is as high as the top of the capstone. Several large, seemingly upright stones can be seen beneath the capstone, but it is difficult to say with any certainty which of these belong to the tomb's structure. A short distance to the south of the monument's location there is a prominent rocky outcrop, a feature that is something of a theme with many of Waterford's portal tombs.

Two kilometres south-east there is a standing stone in **Ballingarry**, lying where it fell, in the centre of a field. It is presumably the victim of cattle that used it as a scratching post.

To the east of Kill village, 2 kilometres north of Ballingarry, there are two standing stones in **Killbarrymeaden** TD. One of these is close to the road, to the east of Kill village, in an unused field. Access to this stone is limited, but its small size means that this doesn't really cause a problem.

Moving 4 kilometres to the north there is a stone pair at Lissahane. The tallest of these stones stands over 3.5 metres in height. A second slightly shorter stone lies on the ground nearby.

The Ordnance Survey map shows two more standings stones in Carrickanure TD, 6 kilometres north of *Savagetown* and 2 kilometres north-east of Lissahane, but these, according to a local farmer, are now fallen or removed. These stones stood within 200 metres of a large rath in the same townland. The rath can be seen from the road to the east of the site.

---

* The word 'ditch' is used in the Irish countryside to denote any field boundary and is, more often than not, a raised bank.

Above: Ballynageeragh portal tomb from Du Noyer's 1860s report.

Below: Plan of Ballynageeragh portal tomb.

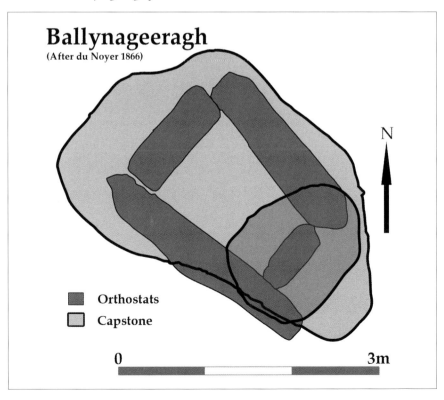

Ballynageeragh
(After du Noyer 1866)

N

Orthostats
Capstone

0   3m

In *Ballyhussa* TD, 4.5 kilometres westward, there used to be a tall, slender standing stone. It was still standing in 2002, but was no longer visible by mid-2007. This stone was over 2 metres tall and just 15 centimetres thick. The field it stood in is used for cattle and its delicate form would not have withstood much use as a scratching post.

Another of the county's portal tombs is 5.5 kilometres to the north in **Whitestown East**. This is very difficult to see properly, because it is built into a field boundary and usually hidden by vegetation. The large, circular capstone measures 4 metres by 3 metres and rests on a few upright stones. The monument is located in the base of a small valley, just 75 metres from the river that runs through it.

In *Ballyquin* TD, 3.5 kilometres south-east of Carrick-on-Suir, there are two fine monuments. The first is a semi-collapsed, but still attractive, portal tomb. The 4-metre-long capstone is supported at one end by two 1.5-metre-tall portal stones. These are unusual, because they are perpendicular to the tomb's axis. The other end of the capstone rests on the ground, making it look similar to Revd R. H. Ryland's 1824 drawing of the now-collapsed portal tomb **Ballindud** TD. However, Ryland's drawing also shows another structural stone, implying that **Ballindud** wasn't always like that, so perhaps the **Ballyquin** portal tomb was originally more substantial. There is a standing stone to the west of the tomb. Early accounts of the site say that there were two tombs here – is this standing stone all that remains of the other tomb? On the south side of the stream, near to the road, there is a Holy Well that sprouts from beneath the roots of a large tree.

The second of these fine monuments in **Ballyquin** TD, 1 kilometre north-east of the portal tomb, is an 'oghamised' standing stone. This now stands just inside a field gate, but it used to stand to the west in the centre of the field. It is over 2 metres tall and is inscribed down its south-west edge. This is slightly hidden by the neighbouring hedgerow.

Another 'oghamised' standing stone can be found just 1 kilometre to the north on a south-facing plateau in *Crehanagh* TD. This damaged stone is 2 metres tall and has inscriptions down its two adjacent southern edges. Immediately to the north, dominating the site, is a large rocky hill. To the west the views extend as far as the Monavullagh Mountains.

Near to the ruins of the monastic settlement at Mothel, one of Waterford's most enigmatic prehistoric artefacts was discovered incorporated into a wall. This is the only piece of rock art ever found in the county. The story of its discovery, loss and then rediscovery is possibly the strangest of any megalithic relic. In 1907 Revd P. Power told of the stone's discovery:

When discovered, on the farm of Mr. John Sheenan, at Mothel, near Carrick-on-Suir, Co. Waterford, the inscribed block formed [a] portion of a rough dry stone fence. Strangely enough the first person to notice it appears to have been – not a farm hand or antiquarian – but a mighty hunter, the late Marquis of Waterford,

Ballyquin portal tomb.

whose attention it attracted as he rode by on a hunting expedition. Was ever [an] antiquarian monument so strangely discovered! His Lordship called the farmer's attention to the block. Notwithstanding this, however, the stone remained neglected – built into the dry stone 'gap', till Mr Sheehan brought it under the writer's notice, some six or seven years since. After exhibition here to-day, it is proposed to deposit this venerable and rude specimen of early Celtic art in the National Museum, Kildare Street.[22]

However, after its exhibition it seemed to have disappeared. It was not lodged at the National Museum. In 1996, S. Johnston published an article mentioning this stone as being mislaid. In response, Elizabeth Shee Twohig (Queen of Megalithic Art) published a short paper stating that the stone was in fact given to University College Cork and put on display in the Stone Corridor, where it can be seen today alongside several ogham stones.[23]

There is yet another portal tomb close to Carrick-on-Suir in **Sheskin** TD, 2.5 kilometres to the south-east of the town. Like **Whitestown East**, this is ruinous. However, unlike **Whitestown East** it is next to a track and easy to see. All that remains is the large displaced capstone, the two portal stones and the doorstone, and one side stone from the chamber. The portals and doorstone are still upright, but their incorporation into a ditch makes them difficult to see properly. Several old palettes lean against them, hiding them further. Isabel Grubb first brought the Sheskin portal tomb to the attention of the establishment in a small paper in 1944,

Mothel rock art after
Revd P. Power.

where it was referred to as The Dolmen in the Glen. As well as describing the
portal tomb she also described an oval setting of stones surrounding a central cist
and a 2-metre-tall monolith in the same townland.[24]

One and a half kilometres east of **Sheskin**, in **Ballindysert** TD, on a wide plateau, but surrounded by trees that block its views, are a pair of stones. Whether
these were always a twosome, or were once a stone row that was damaged, is not
certain. Today, two large stones stand 15 metres apart on a north-west to south-
east alignment. Their size and this distance do hint at there once being more
stones here.

The area immediately to the east of the Monavullagh and Comeragh
Mountains is a hotspot for bullaun stones. The two most accessible sites are at
Park and **Kilbrack** to the south of the R678 Clonmel to Rathgormack road
between Parkbeg and **Graigavalla**. The bullaun stones at both locations have
been moved from their original positions. The **Park** stone now leans against a
small thicket near a very early Christian site and close to a stream. As bullauns
are often associated with streams it is likely that the bullaun stone predates the
Christian settlement.

Kilbrack was also an early Christian site, which was probably erected there
because of the bullaun stones that were present. These are now incorporated into
a semicircular section of field bank that once surrounded the church, of which no
trace survives above ground. Only one of the three bullaun stones is visible today.
This is a large slab, 1.5 metres by 1 metre, with two basins.

CAPSTONE

N

tree

Sheskin
(after Isabel Grubb 1944)

Plan of Sheskin
portal tomb.

A little over 2 kilometres south of **Kilbrack**, there is a fallen standing stone in **Graigavalla** TD. This lies in a barley field to the rear of some farm buildings. Assuming that it was set quite shallowly, it would have stood not much taller than 1.5m. It was used as a scratching post within recent memory, which accounts for its current state.

Separated from the Monavullagh and Comeragh Mountains by 3 kilometres is a round hill that is the focus of a group of standing stones. The cairn-topped **Croughaun Hill** is 6 kilometres north of Kilmacthomas and is a very prominent landmark in the area. On the west side of the hill there is a standing stone in **Kilclooney** TD and, in **Ashtown** TD, there is a stone pair and a single standing stone. In the fields around these monuments there used to be several more standing stones, but these either fell or were removed.[25] The stone pair is marked on the Ordnance Survey map as a single standing stone. A field wall separates the two stones, but each is easily visible from the other. Both are different types of stone: the western stone is a quartz-grained granite, while the other is a pebble-rich pudding stone.

The solitary stone to the south of the pair is shaped like a wedge standing on end. To the west of both **Ashtown** sites the Monavullagh Mountains form a solid wall. To the north-east Croughaun Hill sits proudly on the horizon.

South of **Ashtown**, in **Kealfoun** TD, there is a standing stone located in a field to the rear of the national school, 300 metres south-east of the church. It is difficult to see from the road as it is immediately next to the rear wall of the playground.

Its top can just be seen over the top of the wall. There is an inscription dated 1931 on its southern face, along with several simple crosses.

North-east of **Kealfoun** stands one of County Waterford's hidden treasures: a stone row in **Rathmaiden** TD. Like the **Ashtown** stone pair this six-stone stone row is incorrectly labelled on the Ordnance Survey map. It is also marked as being 200 metres wide of its actual location. The row stands on a broad plateau to the south-east of Croughaun Hill. It is aligned south-east to north-west and points to a spot on the southern slopes of the hill. Four of the six stones still stand, while the other two stones lie prostrate where they fell. A hedgerow runs parallel to the alignment, just 1.5 metres to the north. Its bushes are now engulfing the stones and ivy is also slowly covering some of the stones. Soon this monument may well disappear into the hedgerow completely.

Four kilometres to the south-west of Kilmacthomas, and 500 metres north of the N25, there are a pair of 'oghamised' standing stones at **Garranmillon Lower**. Again, these are marked incorrectly on the Ordnance Survey map (1st series). These 2-metre-tall stones stand 1.5 metres apart on a south-east to north-west alignment and both bear an ogham inscription on their north-west edge. To the east there is an unusually placed sub-rectangular enclosure. This is built onto a north-facing slope and used to be a church site. Only a small rectangular-stone platform remains of the church.

To the south-east of **Garranmillon Lower** there is a very interesting site. At **Drumlohan** there is a souterrain, which probably dates back to the Iron Age. Many of the lintels forming the roof, and several of the orthostats that form the underground structure's walls, bear ogham inscriptions. The roof-stones that are inscribed now stand next to the partially open souterrain inside a small fenced enclosure. It was found when a section of the embankment of a rath, which surrounded a smaller killeen or circular enclosure, was destroyed. Sir Samuel Fergusson recorded the site in detail while the roof-stones were still in place. The fact that the ogham inscriptions were partly obscured indicated that they originally stood elsewhere and had been reused:

> The stones forming the side walls and roof almost all bear Ogham legends, but, having been inscribed before they were turned to this use, have for the most part portions of their texts concealed.[26]

There is no apparent trace of the rest of the outer rath's banks visible today, but the site was clearly an important one. Fergusson thought that the chronological relationship of the monuments was that the inner killeen came first and 'housed' the ogham stones, then the outer rath was constructed and the ogham stones were robbed from the inner site and used in the construction of the souterrain. This may be so, but the inner enclosure could originally have been a small rath around which a larger rath was constructed, perhaps when the residents rose in status. It is possible that the ogham stones could have been trophies collected

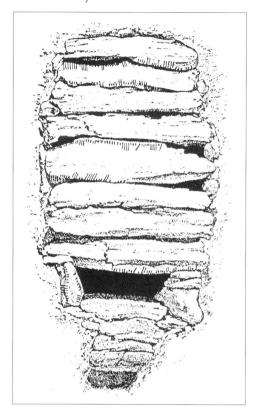

Nineteenth-century drawing of Drumlohan souterrain before its excavation and the removal of the inscribed lintels.

from local sites conquered during this rise in status, and may not have all come from this site initially.

Just east of Ballyvoyle, 5.5 kilometres south of **Drumlohan**, in **Sheskin** TD, there is a small standing stone. It is 1.2 metres tall, but is difficult to see, as the field in which it stands is behind a barbed-wire-topped gate with large 'Private Property' signs attached to it.

The Monavullagh and Comeragh Mountains

The mountain range that runs from north to south through County Waterford is split into two: the Comeragh Mountains at the north and the Monavullagh Mountains to the south, although there is no distinct geographical boundary between the two sections. The northern slopes of the Comeragh Mountains drop to the flood plains of the River Suir to the east of Clonmel. The distance from the base of these slopes to the river is less than 1 kilometre, so this region is included in this section. To the south, the foothills of the Monavullagh Mountains reach the plains below, 5 kilometres north of Dungarvan. There are no monuments within the area that match the criteria for inclusion in this book. However, for the sake of completeness the region is included in this section. This makes the area covered by this section into a band that stretches from the county border next to Clonmel and the coast east of Dungarvan.

On the flood plains of the River Suir in **Gurteen Lower** TD a portal tomb and a standing stone can be found. The standing stone is at the base of the northern slopes of the Comeragh foothills. It is 1.5 metres tall with an uneven profile. The portal tomb, 2 kilometres to the west, is difficult to see as it has become very over-grown in the last fifteen to twenty years. The trees that protected it for so long have fallen, allowing the sunlight to reach the woodland floor. This has enabled a thick layer of brambles to cover the ground and the tomb. Hidden beneath the undergrowth, the remains of the tomb consist of the three orthostats that form the chamber and an upright portal stone – the other portal stone has fallen. The capstone has been displaced and leans against the other stones.

In the neighbouring townland of **Gurteen Upper**, 3 kilometres south of the portal tomb, there is a 3-metre-tall standing stone. Sadly, the true magnificence of this stone cannot be appreciated, because it stands in a modern pine plantation. It is located next to a track in the woods, but the trees adjacent to it almost hide it.

The first three peaks down the east side of the Comeragh Mountains, travel-ling north to south, are Shauneenabreaga, Knocksheegowna and Knockanaffrin. These rise in height from 600 metres to 755 metres. On a spur on the west side of Knockanaffrin Mountain, in **Knockanaffrin** TD, there is a north-east- to south-west-aligned stone row. It has three stones, two of which are 1.7 metres tall and the other is just 40 centimetres tall. This arrangement is very unusual, as the stones in a stone row normally rise consistently in height. The two taller stones are set 1.5 metres apart, while the smaller stone is 4 metres away. The view to the west along the Nier Valley is breathtaking. To the east Knockanaffrin Mountain rises steeply and looms ominously over the site. Also in **Knockanafrrin** TD, 400 metres to the west of the stone row, there is an axial stone circle. This is not marked on the Ordnance Survey map, nor is it in the *Archaeological Inventory of County Waterford*. The author discovered this site after getting lost on the way to visit the stone row. It is built on a small shelf below a steep, rock-covered slope. The stones are only just visible above the ground surface, but its 15-metre diameter can be traced and the axial stone at the south west is discernible.

At the head of the Nier Valley, 1.5 kilometres south-east of **Knockanaffrin** in **Carrigeen** TD, there is a 2-metre-tall standing stone. This may be an ancient route marker for the track that leads from the top of the valley over the mountains through a high pass called The Gap. Below it there is a large burnt mound or *fulacht fia* – the remains of a prehistoric cooking site.

Overlooking the Nier Valley from its southern slopes there is a complex of monuments in **Tooreen** and **Tooreen West** TDs. Pine trees surround the sites here, including a stone circle, a stone row and a pair of barrows. Despite this they are quite easy to find, because there is a signposted trail around the woods. The first site on the trail is the stone circle, which is in **Tooreen** TD. This is set in a small clearing

Knockanaffrin stone row.

Looking along the Nire Valley past Carrigeen standing stone.

not much larger than its 6-metre diameter. Most of its stones are present, although a few of them have fallen. Second on the trail is the stone row in **Tooreen West** TD. This is aligned north-west to south-east and has three stones. The tallest of these, at the northwest end, is just over 1 metre tall. The other stones then decrease in height to 40 centimetres tall. As at the nearby stone circle, trees encroach too heavily on this monument, completely obstructing what must be splendid views over the Nier Valley. Hopefully, when the trees around the stone row are felled, enough room will be created to allow the site to come to life. Site three on the trail is a low barrow, also in **Tooreen West** TD. The ditch around it is just visible and it has an associated stone row next to it. The stones in this row are no more than 30 centimetres tall.

South of the Tooreen complex lies the meeting point of the Comeragh and the Monavullagh Mountains, and this region is barren of sites, either that or its remoteness means that it is under-explored and there are sites up there yet to be discovered.

In **Cutteen North** TD, on the peak of Seefin Mountain, one of the highest peaks in the range, there is a cairn. This has been heavily disturbed, revealing a cist at its centre. The cairn material has been arranged around the edge of the monument to provide shelter for walkers. One hundred metres north of the cairn there is a rock outcrop. Weathering and erosion has caused this to break up into large blocks. Many of these blocks appear to be arranged into lines, but this could be a natural phenomenon.

Eight hundred metres south-east of the cairn, in **Cutteen North** TD, there is another cairn in the neighbouring townland of **Cutteen South**. This 8-metre-diameter cairn is located on the crest of a ridge that runs south-east from the peak of Seefin Mountain and overlooks the Bearna na Madra gap, the col or saddle between Seefin and Farbreaga Mountains.

At the lowest point of this col there is a 2-metre-tall standing stone, which rests on the boundary between **Cutteen South** and **Coumaraglinmountain** TDs. It is aligned east-west and has a rectangular cross section. The southern face has been whitewashed. A short distance to the south there is a large drystone-walled enclosure.

To the west of the standing stone, in the tongue-twistingly named **Scartnadrinnymountain** TD, there is a cluster of three denuded cairns. These cairns are situated in a shallow saddle between a rocky outcrop to the south and a towering cliff to the north. Due to bracken and thigh-high heather, two of the cairns are difficult to see, but the third rises high enough to make it stand out clearly. As recently as 1993 one of the cairns was damaged by forestry work.

To the south-west of **Scartnadrinnymountain**, on a small spur of land overlooking the Araglin River, there is a stone pair in **Kilbrien Lower** TD. This is not quite aligned south-east to north-west with the tallest stone at the south-east end. The alignment is a little south of what you would expect here: an exact north-east to south-west alignment would point directly at the Maum Pass, but the stone actually points to the southern slope of Crohaun Mountain.

Cutteen South/Coumaraglinmountain standing stone from the west.

Below the **Cutteen South** standing stone, towards the head of the Araglin Valley, there is a large complex of sites mainly in **Coumaraglinmountain** TD. Many of the monuments in this area are standing stones less than 1 metre in height, which are not included in the gazetteer. Amongst these sites there are two stone circles, several cairns, a barrow and a possible henge. They are split into two distinct groups, which are now separated by a remote farmhouse. The stone circles are small and ruinous, just 3-4 metres in diameter. A pair of cairns in the northern group of these monuments are very interesting: both have central cists and a standing stone set to the west. Many of the monuments here seem to be orientated towards the west, which is hardly surprising as all the views in other directions are blocked by tall mountains. The southern stone circle has a small outlier to the northwest that points towards the cairns at **Scartnadrinnymountain**.

In **Treenearla Commons** TD, 1.5 kilometres to the south-east of the above groups, there is another smaller complex of monuments. Three cairns and a 2-metre-tall standing stone make up this complex. Two of the cairns are quite large, but both have been robbed to some degree. The other is now buried below the peat. There is no shortage of stones for building cairns in the vicinity: the ground around these sites is littered with small boulders. The standing stone is situated alongside an ancient trackway that leads up towards Farbreaga Mountain to the north-east. These monuments overlook the Maum Pass, a road that passes across the Monavullagh Mountains between Crohaun and Farbreaga Mountains.

Treenearla Commons cairn from the south, with Farbreaga Mountain behind.

Crohaun Mountain from the west.

On the top of **Crohaun** there is a very large cairn. It is 30 metres in diameter and 3 metres high. No kerbstones are visible, but its hilltop position does imply that it could be a passage tomb. In the 1980s a large concrete cross was erected on top of the cairn. It was painted bright white and light blue. The Ordnance Survey trig point that also stands on top of the cairn has been painted blue. The views from the top of **Crohaun** spread out in every direction. To the south is Dungarvan Bay and to the north are the Monavullagh Mountains on the opposite side of the Maum Pass. Eastwards lie the plains of east Waterford, while to the west are the Knockmealdown Mountains.

West Waterford

After leaving the mountains and heading west towards County Cork the monuments begin to thin out. There is just one tomb in this region; the remainder of the monuments are predominantly standing stones and stone rows. At **Reanadampaun Commons** the first of the stone rows can be found on a plateau to the south-west of Milk Hill. Its six stones are incorporated into a field boundary and are aligned north-east to south-west. The tallest stone is no more than 1.3 metres in height. The order of the stones is a little peculiar: they do not seem to be arranged in a predictable sequence. Starting at the south-west there are two large, uneven stones, followed by a partially dressed stone with a square section, a small, pointed stone, a square-sectioned stone and, finally, another small, pointed stone. The question must be asked whether they have been moved. Effectively, there are three pairs of stones that decrease in size, starting with the uneven stones. Could these have originally formed a stone circle? If a seventh, wide stone were added to these they would be perfect for an axial stone circle. Its alignment along a common axis for stone rows may be coincidental.

Due west of Milk Hill, in **Castlereagh** TD, are a pair of ring barrows. The southerly one of these has been disturbed by a field boundary. The other is a fine example with a clearly defined bank and low, central mound. The location offers a splendid vista to the west that is dominated by the Knockmealdown Mountains. A line drawn through these two barrows, if extended in a south-easterly direction, would cross the Monavullagh Mountains very close to the Maum Pass and Crohaun Mountain, which is visible from the site.

Four kilometres to the south of **Reanadampaun Commons** in **Knockboy** TD there is another stone row. This has just three stones that are aligned north-east to south-west. These decrease in height, with the tallest stone at the south-west. A fourth stone lies prostrate nearby that might have been an outlying standing stone associated with the row. Six hundred metres to the south-west of the stone row is Knockboy church. Anyone in this area should definitely stop there and take a look at the many ogham stones that are incorporated into the church's structure as window and door lintels.

There is a large concentration of sites around An Rinn, the peninsula to the south of Dungarvan. Three and a half kilometres to the south of Ringville, in *Lagnagoushee* TD, there is a fallen standing stone. This is very similar to the example at *Boherboy*, 5 kilometres to the south-east alongside the N25. Both the *Boherboy* and *Lagnagoushee* stones have fallen. They are thick stones: over 1 metre deep and wide. It is difficult to say how tall the latter was, but the *Boherboy* stone stood upright until as recently as 2003.[27] Their locations are also very similar, on the top of low, wide rises with extensive, yet mainly featureless views in all directions.

Between the two stones above there is a fine standing stone in *Ahaun* TD. When viewed from the road this looks a little unusual, because of the concrete Ordnance Survey trig point that has been erected just 2 metres away from it. The stone is over 2 metres tall and very rough. It is a 40-centimetre-thick slab with a base 1 metre across. It increases in width to 1.5 metres and then tapers to a point. Being located at one of the highest points in the area the views are wonderful, except where blocked by the pine plantation to the south-west.

Beyond the plantation, 500 metres to the south-west of *Ahaun*, there is a smaller standing stone in *Monaneea* TD. This is a much nicer stone than the former, but it is significantly smaller. It has a very uniform profile and plan. It is 1.5 metres tall with a round top. It stands between two young pine plantations in a very soggy field, which is divided up by a maze of electric fences.

Continuing south-west for 2 kilometres brings us to *Glenwilliam*, where, in a field next to a road junction, we encounter another standing stone. This is similar in size to that at *Monaneea*, but is not at all uniform in profile or plan.

Five and a half kilometres east-north-east of *Monaneea* there are two standing stones in Ballynamona Upper TD marked on the Ordnance Survey map. The most westerly of these appears to have disappeared. A house now stands close to where it is marked, so the garden's high hedges may be hiding the stone. Both stones are said to be, or to have been, over 2 metres tall.

It is quite interesting to look at the layout of the stones mentioned so far on the Ordnance Survey map. For those that like ley-lines there are several long-distance alignments between these stones. A line through the two *Ballynamona Upper* stones passes close to the *Lagnagoushee* standing stone. Extending a line through the *Ahaun* and *Monaneea* stones passes through the one at *Glenwilliam*. The *Lagnagoushee*, *Ahaun* and *Boherboy* standing stones are also on a line. Lines through *Boherboy* and the southernmost stone in *Ballynamona Upper* on the one hand, and *Ahaun* and the northernmost stone in *Ballynamona Upper* on the other, converge to cross very close to the court tomb at *Ballynamona Lower*.

The court tomb at *Ballynamona Lower* is another of the county's best-kept secrets. Its fairly remote location and lack of signposts means that very few people ever visit it. The site's importance becomes apparent when you consider that it is one of only three confirmed court tombs in the south of Ireland. The other two are at Shanballyedmond (County Tipperary) and Farnoge (County Kilkenny).

Ahaun standing stone and the Ordnance Survey trig point that stands next to it.

The Farnoge monument is a double court tomb, but the one at Shanballyedmond is very similar to the **Ballynamona Lower** example. At **Ballynamona Lower** the gallery is 4 metres long and has a gabled back-stone. All the orthostats forming the gallery are present, but the court is much denuded. The location is dramatic: near to the edge of a high cliff overlooking the south Waterford coast, which stretches ahead to the east. To the south the lighthouse at Mine Head is visible.

The **Ballynamona Lower** court tomb was excavated in 1938 by a team led by T.G.E. Powell as part of the Relief of Unemployment scheme operated by the Office of Public Works and the National Museum. The west-facing forecourt was found to be paved with a layer of clay. This floor was covered by a layer of tightly packed cairn material, presumably the last act of sealing up the tomb after the final time it was used. The gallery is 3 metres long and made from five orthostats: two for each side and a backstone. The entrance is defined by two opposing jambs with a 50-centimetre gap between them. A single orthostat divides the gallery in two. This extends across two thirds of the gallery from the north wall. A small sill stone occupies the gap that is left by this stone. None of the orthostats were set into the ground when it was constructed. They stand directly on the old ground surface with smaller stones packed around their bases for stability. At the time of the excavation it was reported that locals could remember treasure seekers digging into the floor of one of the chambers.

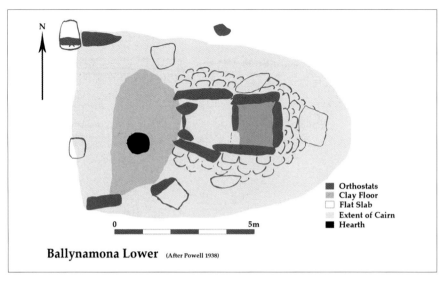

Plan of Ballynamona Lower court tomb.

Finds from the excavation were surprisingly good considering the amount of disturbance inside the tomb. These included some beautifully decorated sherds from a bowl estimated to have been 13 centimetres in diameter. An amount of flint flakes were found in the chambers and amongst the cairn material. Only three of these could be identified as having once been worked. An old red Sandstone disc, 5 centimetres in diameter, was found in the rear chamber. The excavation report notes that larger examples of such discs have been found in tombs in Brittany, Scotland, Wales and at Moylisha, County Wicklow.[28]

South of **Ballynamona Lower**, inside the ruined church at the base of Ardmore round tower, there is a collection of ogham stones. None of these qualify as being megalithic, but local folklore does hold some tantalising clues to ancient worship at stones in the area. The following is an account by Revd R. H. Ryland:

> The parish of Ardmore was anciently a place of some consequence, the favourite retreat of St Declan, the friend and companion of St Patrick. … 'St Declan's Stone' is on the beach; it is a large rock, resting on two others which elevate it a little above the ground. On the 24th July, the festival of the saint, numbers of the lowest class do penance on their bare knees around the stone, and some, with great pain and difficulty, creep under it, in expectation of thereby curing or preventing, what it is much more likely to create rheumatic affections of the back.[29]

The reverend obviously considered this a pagan practice and disapproved, but was still able to put a humorous slant on his opinion. W.G. Wood–Martin, nearly seventy later, gave a slightly more elaborate version of the practice:

Pottery sherds from Ballynamona Lower – After Kilbride-Jones.

> The 'Cloch-Nave-Deglane' lies amongst the boulders on the strand at Ardmore, and
> it used to be the centre of great attraction on St Declan's patron day. The pilgrims,
> after performing their 'rounds', squeezed themselves through under it three times.
> This stone is noted for several cures, especially pains of the back; it is a belief that no
> one with borrowed or stolen clothes can pass unharmed under it.[30]

It is not difficult to find this relic, but its significance seems to have been lost in
time: even during Ardmore's Pattern Weekend Festival it does not feature as an
attraction. At the west end of Ardmore strand there is an area of rocks slightly
separated from the main beach. It can be accessed by a set of steps. In the centre
of this area is St Declan's Stone. Sadly one end of the balanced stone of St Declan
has slipped from its support.

Wood-Martin then wrote of a second stone of interest in Ardmore that sounds
as if it was a bullaun stone:

> Another famous stone at Ardmore has been buried, probably for the purpose of
> putting an end to its attendant ceremonies, as it must be classed among those relics
> connected with rites of days long gone by. It was called the 'Cloch-Daha' – stated
> to signify 'the Stone of the Dagda'. It was about 2 feet long by 18 inches in breadth
> and same in depth, hollowed out into an oval trough-like shape, probably an old
> Pagan 'rock basin'! Its centre was pierced by a hole, in which, on Ash Wednesday,
> the young unmarried men of the village inserted a wattle, on the top of which they
> tied a quantity of tow. They then brought with them all the unmarried maidens

they could muster from the village and vicinity, and made them dance around the Cloch-Daha, holding the pendant tow, and spinning it whilst dancing. The ceremony terminated by the young men dragging the maidens through the village seated on logs of wood.[31]

This sounds like a pagan fertility ceremony, so it is understandable that, in more prudish and puritanical times, someone took action and prevented it from taking place. Dancing around a stick with ribbons tied to it resembles maypole dancing in England, long thought to be the relic of an ancient fertility dance.

North of these stones, 8 kilometres west of Dungarvan in *Kilgreany* TD, is one of Ireland's most important cave sites. It was excavated in 1928 and again in 1934. Finds from these digs ranged from elk bones to a gaming die. Two inhumations were discovered that were originally thought to be from the Palaeolithic period, but radiocarbon dating in 1993 established their burial date to be around 4500 BCE. A reassessment of the excavation finds from the cave concluded that the cave was used for burial purposes in the Neolithic and Bronze Age, and later became a votive-offering site in the Late Bronze Age. A total of twenty-two people are thought to be represented by the remains recovered, several of which show signs of trauma caused by blows from a sharp edge.[32]

Moving north again to Dyrick Hill, 6 kilometres east of *Knockboy*, there is a cluster of three standing stones in *Dyrick*, *Mweeling* and *Doon* TDs. The most northerly of these, in *Doon* TD, is the tallest at 1.85 metres. The *Mweeling* stone stands 1.2 metres tall on a small plateau to the north of Dyrick Hill. A steep rise to the west, the start of the Knockmealdown Mountains, blocks the views in that direction. To the east the view extends to the Monavullagh Mountains. The *Dyrick* stone is a peculiar one. It is 1.8 metres tall and looks like a model of a skyscraper: it is made up of rectangular sections of varying heights. It is now surrounded by pine trees, but at one time the cairn-topped Dyrick Hill, just 500 metres to the east, would have dominated the site.

On the summit of Knocknafallia Mountain, the third highest peak in the Knockmealdown Mountains, there is an unusual, if not unique, cairn in *Glennafallia* TD. This is over 10 metres in diameter and a little over 1.5 metres in height. Its ten visible kerbstones are placed so that alternate ones are set radially: that is they alternate between following the circumference of the cairn and pointing outwards from the centre like spokes. The centre has been hollowed out slightly, probably by hill walkers to provide shelter. On the north-western edge of the cairn there is a 1-metre-tall standing stone, at the base of which is a spread of large quartz blocks. Diametrically opposite this, facing south-east, there is an open-fronted kist. This is half filled with cairn material, amongst which many small quartz pebbles can be seen. The open entrance of this chamber faces directly towards *Crohaun*.

St Declan's Stone on Ardmore strand.

The Glennafallia cairn on top of Knocknafallia Mountain, with the 794-metre-high peak of Knockmealdown Mountain beyond.

Megalithic Monuments

'What is a Cromleac? If I was asked this question by a critical antiquary, I could not answer it to his satisfaction, nor could he to my own.' — George Du Noyer, 1846.

'Megalithic' is one of those adjectives that does exactly what is says on the box. It derives from two Greek words: *mega* meaning large and *líthos* meaning stone. Obviously, the term megalithic monument is a very broad one, which covers all types of prehistoric sites created through the use of large stones, and so, to make things easier, this broad classification has been broken down into subcategories such as 'standing stones', 'stone circles', 'passage tombs' and so on (all of which will be discussed in further detail below). All of these different categories have their own defining features, some of which are incredibly obvious, some of which are more subtle. With the exception of the barrows and some of the standing stones, the monuments in this book date from the period known as the Neolithic or New Stone Age. The beginning of the Neolithic period in Ireland was pushed back in the late 1990s from 3500 BCE to 5500 BCE with the use of radiocarbon dating on the tombs at Carrowmore in Sligo. It ended in around 2000 BCE with the start of the Bronze Age.

For visiting ancient sites I recommend using the Ordnance Survey (OS) maps. When looking at an Ordnance Survey map you will see most of the historical sites marked by a red dot with an accompanying categorical title. The ones that concern this book are 'Artificial Mound', 'Barrow', 'Bullaun Stone', 'Cairn', 'Standing Stone(s)', 'Stone Circle', 'Stone Row' and 'Megalithic Tomb'. The addition of 'Bullaun Stone' to this list is my own. Bullaun stones are not generally accepted as being megalithic monuments, but I will argue their case later on. 'Megalithic Tomb' is a generic term, which covers many different types of sepulchral monument – court tombs, kists, passage tombs, portal tombs and wedge tombs. The differences between these types will also be described shortly. Most people know these types of monument by the terms cromlech or dolmen. The use of the word 'tomb' in these names is becoming a contested one, mainly because excavations are beginning to show that relatively sparse remains were interred within most of these monuments. The scarcity of human remains in many (but not all) of these monuments has been attributed to the acidic soil found in most parts of Ireland, which may be the case, but this lack of evidence is beginning to lead some to reconsider the role that the monuments played in the lives of the Ancients who built them. They are now starting to be looked at more as a ritual building with a much broader purpose, perhaps closer to modern churches than some would like to believe.

Monument Types That Appear in This Book

★ Although similar to the same section in *Monu-Mental About Prehistoric Dublin*, this section has been revised to reference Waterford-based sites.

Artificial Mounds

Across the country there are many man-made mounds that are not classified as barrows, mottes or passage tombs mainly because they have never been properly explored.

The vast majority of artificial mounds are round in plan and hemispherical in shape or truncated cones. These could be sod-covered cairns or simply piles of earth. Occasionally they are rectangular in plan with flat tops. Every one of them could be a burial monument, but some are likely to have been built as either viewing platforms or to mark the location of a long-forgotten event, such as a battle.

Until each site is individually researched their purpose will never be certain.

Barrows

Although barrows are not Neolithic, and certainly not megalithic in most cases, they are included here because their location can tell us a lot about habitation areas in the Neolithic and the period immediately following – the Bronze Age. In their most common form they consist of a raised earthen mound, which is often surrounded by a fosse (a ditch around a monument) and bank.

Unfortunately, the fact that barrows tended to be built near to habitation sites has its negative side too, because it means that they are often located on good-quality land. This has led to many of them being ploughed away and they can be difficult to identify, especially from the ground. A great many potential sites are identified from aerial photography through crop marks, a distinctive change in the appearance of a crop when viewed from the air by the underlying monument altering soil conditions above it.

The area covered by a barrow can vary from as little as 5 metres to over 30 metres in diameter, but the average is in the region of 10-15 metres. Due to erosion and damage caused by ploughing it is difficult to define a typical height for barrows, but some of the better-preserved large examples approach 3 metres tall.

Burial rite is usually a single inhumation or a cremated burial. The burials are generally centrally placed, either in a pit or in a stone- or wood-lined chamber

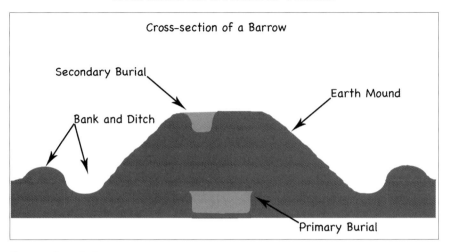

Cross-section of a Barrow

Secondary Burial

Earth Mound

Bank and Ditch

Primary Burial

Cross section of a barrow.

called a cist, which may or may not be covered by a capstone or wooden lid.
Later, secondary burials are often found inserted into the covering mound.

One interesting contrast between megalithic monuments and barrows is that
barrows often occur in groups or barrow cemeteries. Of the megalithic monuments only passage tombs share this trait.

There are several distinctive designs of barrow. Bell or bowl barrows are the
simplest type – consisting of just a simple round mound. Some examples have a
well-defined bank and ditch, usually referred to as a fosse, encircling them, whereas
others have no fosse or bank. Long barrows are rare in Ireland and more common in England; they are elongated in plan with the burial(s) set towards one end.
The earliest English examples, such as West Kennett, have megalithic chambers.
Pond barrows are another rare style; they are indicated by a waterlogged depression
surrounded by a bank and fosse and are not at all common in Ireland. Ring barrows are more like mini henges; they have no mound, but consist of a flat, circular
area demarked by a bank and fosse. Ring barrows are by far the most common in
Waterford.

Cists/Kists

A cist is a stone- or wood-lined burial chamber that is set into the ground
and often covered by a wooden or stone lid. They are found beneath barrows and cairns, and can contain inhumations or cremations. They date back
to either the Bronze Age or Iron Age. Occasionally, they occur as secondary burials inserted into the cairns of earlier Neolithic monuments. There
is a large example hiding in the undergrowth just inside the entrance to the
enclosure around **Gaulstown** portal tomb that was probably incorporated into
its now-lost long cairn.

The word kist is used to describe small stone burial chambers that are built above ground, and are often covered by a cairn. They are usually four-sided and have a large capstone. Kists are generally Neolithic in date and contain inhumations.

Archaeologists mainly use the word cist to describe both types, but it is easier to make the distinction by using kist for the more megalithic versions.

Court Tombs

Court tombs are considered to be among the earliest forms of megalithic tomb in Ireland. In their most common form, they consist of a long, orthostatic gallery that opens onto a semi-circular area defined by orthostats: the court. The galleries are often segmented into sub-chambers by jambs – orthostats that are set at right angles to the gallery walls, leaving a gap at one side to allow passage into the next chamber. Two large stones known as jambs usually frame the entrance. This simple form is known as a single court tomb. County Waterford's only example of a court tomb, **Ballynamona Lower**, is of this design.

Other variations include the double court tomb and centre court tomb. In double court tombs, two single court tombs are built back to back in the same cairn, with their courts facing in opposite directions. A centre court tomb is created by building two single court tombs with the courts facing each other to create an enclosed central area with a gallery leading off each side.

In all varieties, a heavily corbelled roof would have covered the gallery. To create this type of roof in a court tomb, large slabs are leant against the outside of the gallery orthostats. Then more slabs are leant against these to create an inverted V shape over the gallery. A cairn would have then covered the whole of this structure. It is not unusual to find subsidiary chambers built into the tail of the cairn behind the gallery.

Henges

Although the word 'henge' was originally coined to describe the 'hanging stones' at Stonehenge in Wiltshire, England, the term is now used to categorise a very different monument. Henges are circular, earthen structures created by digging a ditch and raising a bank on the outside. It is common for there to be an entrance on the eastern side, formed by leaving a gap in the bank with a causeway across the internal ditch.

In the majority of cases very little archaeological evidence is uncovered within the enclosed area, leading to the conclusion that they were solely ritual monuments. When excavations do uncover evidence of activity it is often quite unusual. Some monuments that are classed as henges have an external bank, which means that many of Ireland's raths or fortified homesteads could have started out as henges. Some of the larger ring barrows could also be henges.

Passage Tombs

Passage tombs are so-called because the burial chamber is reached via a passage leading from the outer edge of the covering mound or cairn. The walls of the pas-

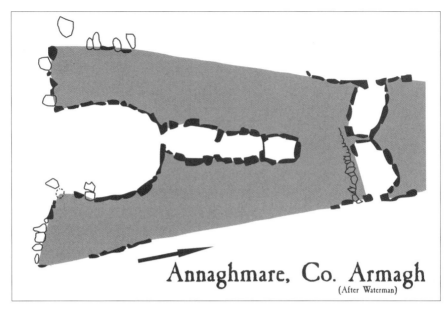

Annaghmare, Co. Armagh
(After Waterman)

Plan of a single court tomb with subsidiary chambers.

sage, like those of the chamber, are usually constructed from large slabs standing up on end known as orthostats, but can be of drystone walling. The roof of the passage is constructed by placing large slabs on the tops of the orthostats. The chamber roof can be either made from similar horizontally laid slabs or by a method called corbelling. Corbelling is the process of placing successive layers of stones on top of each other, decreasing the gap with each layer to reduce the span until only a small opening remains. A single stone is placed across the space to form the last part of the roof. The chamber in Newgrange has one of the finest examples of a corbelled roof.

The internal chambers of passage tombs vary in design. The 'classic' style is the cruciform chamber, where the main chamber has three sub-chambers leading off it, one opposite the passage and one off either side, forming a cross when viewed from above. In others the chamber is little more than a slight widening of the passage. Such examples are called undifferentiated passage tombs. The famous tomb at Newgrange has one of the finest cruciform chambers and Ireland's largest example, Knowth, has both a cruciform and an undifferentiated chamber.

The passage tombs of Waterford form a very special group that have an affinity with those found on the Scilly Isles. These are of the undifferentiated style. Sadly none of them retain their covering cairn, but those at **Matthewstown** and **Harristown** are still exceptional monuments.

Portal Tombs
Whereas passage tombs often occupy the most dramatic locations, portal tombs are, more often than not, situated in more subtle places such as in valleys or at

Harristown passage tomb.

the base of hills. This does not mean, however, that they are not spectacular in their own right, because the general characteristics of the class make them the most visually striking of all the tombs. These are the monuments that are usually referred to as dolmens or cromlechs.

Portal tombs are often grouped together with wedge and court tombs in the larger group of gallery tombs, but the chambers of portal tombs are never sub-divided by jambs or sill stones. A sill stone is a low stone set across the width of an opening and a jamb is a tall stone set against the wall of the chamber opposite another, leaving a space between them.

Whilst the many similarities between the different styles must be considered, this is, in the author's opinion, enough to warrant portal tombs being placed in a class of their own. The main argument is that the portal stones derive from the entrance jambs of court tombs and a small number of portal tombs show some signs of hav-ing a degenerate court such as can be seen at Ahaglaslin (County Cork).

The single chamber is usually formed with just three walls: a single slab forms the rear (the backstone) and in most cases single stones form the two sides of this box-like construction. Set in front of each of the sides is a taller stone, which projects forward occasionally inline with them, but they are more usually set just outside the side stones. Together these form an entrance or a 'portal' and are referred to as portal stones. Between these there is often an inset door stone, which occupies the full width of the portal and forms an alcove. The height of these door stones varies and can be half-, three-quarter- or full-height.

Gaulstown portal tomb.

The structure is finished off with the capstone, a huge slab or block of stone that forms a roof. One end of this rests on the backstone with the other end resting on the portal stones. The front of the capstone projects forwards beyond the portal stones, creating a very dramatic and imposing monument when viewed in profile.

It does not seem to be the case that portal tombs were necessarily incorporated in a mound or cairn, but in many cases evidence of some form of cairn survives. In such cases the monument is placed towards or at one end of a long sub-rectangular cairn. In no surviving instance does the cairn cover the capstone and many believe that portal tombs were never intended to be entirely covered. Given their visually imposing form, this is more than likely. It would appear that the capstones were meant to be left exposed and that the cairn, when present, only served to hide the outside of the chamber walls.

County Waterford has some of the finest portal tombs to be found in Ireland, especially those at **Knockeen** and **Gaulstown**. Fortunately, these are in state care and are easily visited (although the final signpost for **Knockeen** has been missing for some time).

Rock Art
There are two main types of rock art to be found in Ireland: that found decorating flat panels of bedrock or individual standing stones, and the more famous

passage-tomb art found decorating places such as Newgrange, County Meath. When I refer to a site as being rock art I am using the term in the first context: as carved panels or stones.

The motifs used on this type of carving are fairly consistent, although some 'oddball' sites exist. The most common designs are cup marks – a small round depression – and concentric circles. There is only one known example of a spiral carved on a rock panel in Ireland (Rathgeran in County Carlow).

Armed with these two simple elements people have created some fantastic designs. By combining the two, the cup and ring motif is created. Sometimes a gutter is added, which emanates from the central cup mark and cuts through the surrounding rings. The Rathgeran stone mentioned above has two such designs placed side by side, with the gutter connecting the two central cup marks.

Other forms include the rare ladder motif and the cup mark with concentric penannular rings – rings that are broken.

The national distribution of rock art is unknown due to the potential for so much to still be buried below peat deposits. There are large concentrations around the copper-yielding areas of Counties Cork and Kerry as well as in County Donegal. County Louth lost several good groups of panels through field clearance in the late 1900s and many others have been allowed to become overgrown to protect them. The combination of unrecorded loss through destruction and landowners allowing panels to become covered makes visiting rock art a difficult task.

Vast quantities of rock art are being discovered in the UK through the concentrated efforts of amateur rock-art hunters. There is no reason why, with the same sort of dedication, new rock art could not still be found in Ireland. Over recent years a large concentration has been found around Drumirril TD, County Monaghan, for example.

Although there are several possible cup marks on some of Waterford's standing stones, only one piece of 'proper' rock art has been recorded here and this can no longer be found in the county, but now occupies a spot in the Stone Corridor in UCC.[33]

Standing Stones

What name could be more descriptive? Also known as menhirs or monoliths, standing stones are the simplest form, structurally, of megalithic monuments and the most common. They are quite simply stones that have been stood up intentionally by man, with one end set into the ground. However, their original purpose is far from straightforward for they have been erected during many time periods and for many different reasons.

Some were originally boundary markers, others such as the huge Punchestown standing stone (County Kildare) were erected to mark burials, while others marked locations significant to the Ancients and, just to add to the confusion, many were erected in modern times as scratching posts for cattle. Sometimes standing stones are found in association with stone circles. These are known as outliers.

Despite having such a basic form (what can be more basic than a single stone?), standing stones come in a huge array of shapes and sizes and are the most varied of the monuments. At one extreme you have giant, phallic examples such as the Punchestown or Forenaghts Great standing stones (both in County Kildare) and at the other you have small, stumpy ones such as Knockiernan Lower (County Wicklow). Regardless of a stone's size or shape it is often possible to identify why that particular stone was selected. The Glencullen standing stone in County Dublin, for instance, is a beautiful cuboid block of solid quartz. Quartz plays a smaller, less 'in-your-face' role in many standing stones that have thin bands or veins of quartz running through them creating the impression of living rocks complete with veins.

A full range of shapes and sizes of standing stone can be found throughout Waterford, two of the most striking being the Harp Stone in **Whitfield North** TD and the one in **Ballymote** TD.

Stone Circles

Stone circles are just that – stones arranged in a circle – but again it is not that simple: there are many styles of stone circles. In Scotland for instance there are the Recumbent Stone Circles (RSCs) that have a massive altar-like horizontal stone set between two towering flanking stones. In County Cork there are the Axial Stone Circles that have an odd number of stones, usually 5, 7, 11 or 19, where the odd stone is low and broad and the other stones then increase in height as they progress away from this, the axial stone. In County Derry there are stone circles that are made of short stones and often have a tangential stone row of similar stature. Although these localised trends exist, the types are not limited to these areas. This is due to either a migration of ideas or of people, but more study is needed before this can be determined.

Stone circles are the most popular of all the megalithic monuments. It is easy to put this down to being the result of the publicity given to the spectacular solar event at Stonehenge in England or that it is far easier to imagine what a ruined stone circle may have once looked like compared with the effort needed to create a reliable idea of what a ruined tomb was like when it was built, but there is so much more to it than that.

The almost total lack of knowledge about the original purpose of stone circles, or the manner in which they were utilised, allows everyone to speculate and maintain their own fantasy. Several have been found to contain burials, but this does not make them burial monuments. It is more likely that these burials were sacrificial offerings to the gods of the builders, just as it used to be common practice to wall-up a live cat during the construction of houses to ward off evil spirits.

Many purposes have been proposed and in some instances proven. The stone circles at Grange Lios (County Limerick) and Drombeg (County Cork) have confirmed solstice alignments, for example. Proof that a sample had key alignment features does not necessarily mean that they all did. It is this element of the mysterious, coupled with the fascination with the long-forgotten knowledge of the Ancients, that helps to make stone circles so popular. The circle is also the simplest shape to produce and associate with and throughout history it has been used to symbolise the cycle and eternal nature of life and death.

Some of the stone circles listed in this book have been listed in the *Waterford Archaeological Inventory* as 'kerb circles', implying that there was once a cairn raised inside them.

Stone Rows and Stone Pairs

When standing stones are grouped together in a straight line, they become a stone row or an alignment. Two parallel stone rows form an avenue. Stone rows can be very short, with just two stones, or much longer – up to seven stones is quite common in Ireland. Some have even more. As with single standing stones, the shape and size of the stones forming a row can vary greatly, even within a particular stone row. In Cork, for example, it is common for the stones to rise in height from one end to the other.

Occasionally the stones that occur in pairs are separated from the main group of stone rows and referred to as stone pairs. These can often be interpreted as being a male/female pairing because one stone is more slender and phallic in appearance than the other, which is usually more blunt and rounded.

Wedge Tombs

Wedge tombs have a sub-rectangular gallery divided into sub-chambers by low, full-width stones called sill stones or by two full-height stones set opposite each other known as jambs, leaving a narrow gap in between. This latter form is less common and shows a connection with court tombs.

They are called wedge tombs because of their distinctive shape. The front of the monument, which generally faces in a westerly direction, is both wider and taller than its rear.

A single stone spanning the entire width usually blocks the entrance. Two apparently localised trends differ from this rule. The wedge tombs of County Clare tend to have two stones blocking the entrance and those in Northern Ireland often have a single narrow stone centrally placed, which splits the entrance into two halves.

Some, such as Labacallee (County Cork) and Ballyedmonduff (County Dublin), have a sealed-off sub-chamber built onto the rear of the gallery. Other, more

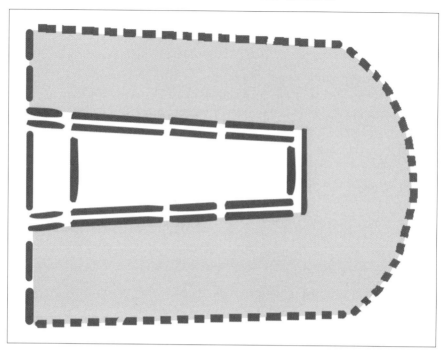

Generic plan of a typical wedge tomb.

common, architectural features also occur, called antechambers and porticos. These are both constructs attached to the front of the gallery, which are basically external sub-chambers. The main difference is that porticos are not closed at the front and are sometimes split in two by a vertical orthostat set along the central axis of the gallery.

The majority of wedge tombs were originally incorporated into a mound or cairn. The more simple structures were usually set into the centre of a round cairn, whereas the monuments with porticos, etc., were often built into a D-shaped mound with the front of the gallery occupying a central position on the flat face. These D-shaped mounds can be quite exaggerated, forming more of a U-shape. It is quite common for the mound to have a small kerb. In a few rare instances more than one gallery was incorporated into a single mound. When this does occur the galleries are always parallel to one another and have their entrances facing in the same direction.

Another question that must be addressed concerns the true role of these structures in the society of their builders. Their portrayal as communal burial places is contradicted by the lack of remains found in the few examples to have been investigated to date. Wedge tombs were built with sealed galleries, whereas the majority of court tombs, portal tombs and passage tombs are constructed to allow repeated access. This would indicate that wedge tombs were final resting places, but perhaps the other types were built as 'mortuary houses', where remains were only placed inside for a short period of time before being removed for disposal elsewhere at a yearly ceremony, for instance. This would certainly help explain the apparent lack of remains found at some sites.

Wedge tombs are by far the most numerous of the 'sepulchral' monuments in Ireland and, unlike all the other megalithic tombs, have a nationwide distribution. They are nearly always located to provide extensive views, usually to the west, but they rarely occupy the highest point in an area. Despite their wide national distribution, wedge tombs are not very common in the south-east: there are only two recognised examples in Waterford (***Carrickavrantry*** and ***Munmahoge***). These, however, are only classed as wedge tombs, because they differ from Waterford's passage tombs. These two monuments, like the passage tombs in the county, have affinities to monuments found on the Isles of Scilly.

Gazetteer Introduction

The gazetteer is organised alphabetically by townland, which to some might be a little confusing as some of these sites are known by other names such as The Harp Stone in *Whitfield North*. I have chosen to use townlands as the primary index because this is how Irish monuments are catalogued in the archaeological inventories. If this practice was more widely used, then cross-referencing sites would be far easier between resources. Where they exist, the common names for monuments are included in the indexes and mentioned in the text.

The author has visited all the sites included, but it should be borne in mind that most of these sites, although under state protection, are on private property and permission to visit should always be sought, unless they are clearly signposted.

Most types of megalithic monument are present in County Waterford, with perhaps the exception of wedge tombs, depending upon the true classification of the two monuments at *Munmahoge* and *Carrickavrantry*. Some are in limited numbers, such as the single court tomb in *Ballynamona Lower* TD and the few stone circles on the Coumeraglin Mountains and in *Tooreen West* TD.

Accompanying each description is the information needed to find the site. For most, directions will be given from the nearest town or landmark, the exceptions being where the directions are simply crazy due to the amount of small roads involved. These directions will get you to the monument, but their presence here does not necessarily mean that there is a right of way. All of the entries will have the grid reference and the ordnance survey map(s) on which the sites can be found. The shape of the south coast means that the Ordnance Survey maps covering the county overlap slightly, so some sites appear on two maps. Where this is the case, both sheets will be listed in the site's entry.

Except for the major places it is recommend that the Ordnance Survey maps are used when planning journeys and for the final approach, but a small word of warning – at the time of writing the road system of Ireland is undergoing so many alterations that often maps are out of date. At this time, the 3rd editions of the Ordnance Survey maps that cover County Waterford have not been published, but are due in 2008. Ordnance Survey maps are available from all good bookstores and from the National Map Centre in Dublin, or directly from the Ordnance Survey of Ireland.

If, through this work, just a handful of people inspired to go out on a Sunday and see some of Ireland's heritage, beyond tourist traps such as Newgrange in County Meath or Poulnabrone in County Clare, then it will have been worthwhile. This is not to demean the importance of Newgrange, but to say that it should be seen as just the beginning and not the end of one's journey into learning about the wondrous monuments left to us by Ireland's early inhabitants.

Notes About Visiting Sites

Most of the monuments in this book are on private land and, no matter how you feel about property being theft and all that, you must respect this when visiting a site. Any damage or nuisance you cause could jeopardise the chances of other people being able to visit.

Always get permission to visit a site if necessary.

When on farmland, take care not to disturb livestock or damage crops.

Leave gates as you find them. If they are shut, shut them after you have passed through. If they are open, leave them open.

Always use paths where available and always walk around the edge of crop fields. Never leave litter behind. THIS INCLUDES TEALIGHTS, CANDLES AND 'OFFERINGS' TO YOUR GODS OF CHOICE. People who visit after you do not want to be confronted with rotting flowers and wax-covered stones. Hot wax is not just unsightly, it also kills the lichen that has taken many, many years to grow.

Take any litter you come across away with you and dispose of it properly. I have returned from some trips with a black bag full of other people's rubbish.

Do not light fires in or near to monuments, you may be destroying unexcavated evidence just below the surface and the resultant burnt-black patches are very unsightly for those that follow you.

Do not remove anything (except for litter) from a site.

Do not chalk in rock art to make it clearer. Take a bottle of water and pour it over the carvings. The reflections will make it just as clear as chalk does and no damage is done to the stones.

Have a thought for others who may be present. You might enjoy loud music while at the stones, but those around you may not.

Enjoy yourself.

One rule sums up all of the above (and more) very nicely:

LEAVE ONLY FOOTPRINTS

AND

TAKE ONLY MEMORIES

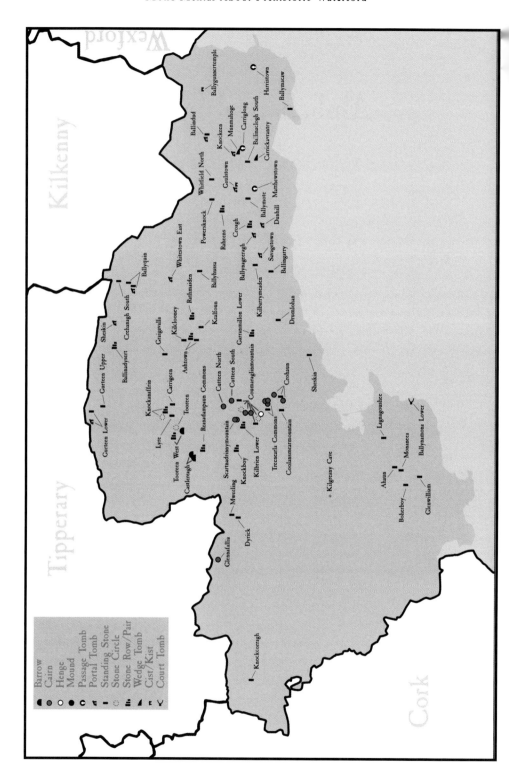

Alphabetical Index

Index by Site Type

Passage Tombs

Portal Tombs

Rock Art

Standing Stones and Ogham Stones

Stone Circles

Stone Rows & Pairs

Wedge Tombs

Gazetteer

Ahaun
Standing Stone
OS Sheet 82: X 228 852

Directions: *Head north from Ardmore on the R673. Turn right at Lisakeelty crossroads approximately 6 kilometres from Ardmore (this is the sixth right turn). Turn left at the next crossroads and continue 2.5 kilometres until you reach a large barn on the right-hand side of the road. The stone can be seen across the fields on the opposite side of the road.*

Unlike the nearby standing stone in **Monaneea** TD, this is a large stone. It stands 2 metres tall and over 1.5 metres across its widest point, where it bulges outwards.

The stone stands at the highest point on a long ridge – a fact attested to by the Ordnance Survey trig point just 2 metres from it. This offers wide views in all directions, which are only broken by a pine plantation to the south.

Mini-Gazetteer – 3.1km SW there is a standing stone in **Glenwilliam**. 6.3km ESE there is Waterford's only court tomb at **Ballynamona Lower**. 2.8km WSW there is a standing stone at **Boherboy**. 13.7km WNW there are some ogham stones at Kiltera.

Ashtown
Standing Stone
OS Sheet 75: S 360 090

Directions: *From Kilmacthomas take the R677 north and turn left at the first opportunity. Turn left again and follow the road, passing a crossroads and a church, for 4 kilometres. Drive up the farm track and ask at the farm for access to the area. There are several standing stones on this land. This one is 500 metres to the south of the farmyard.*

Resembling a huge wedge of petrified cheese, this stone is very similar to one at Piperstown, County Dublin. It is 1.4 metres tall with smooth sides that rise to a fine north-east- to south-west-aligned edge.

Ahaun standing stone, looking west.

Ashtown standing stone, looking west.

To the west Knockaunapeebra and Coumfea Mountains, part of the Monavullagh Mountain range 4 kilometres west, dominate the views. To the north-east the low, sleepy form of Croughaun Mountain rests on the horizon. The top edge of this stone seems to point towards Croughaun, but it does lean slightly, which may mean that any alignment is a coincidence.

Mini-Gazetteer – 7km E there is a standing stone at *Ballyhussa*. 8.7km WNW there is a standing stone at *Carrigeen*. 10.4km NNE there is a portal tomb at *Ballyquin*. 11.1km N there is a portal tomb at *Sheskin*.

Ashtown
Stone Pair
OS Sheet 75: S 363 095

Directions: *From Kilmacthomas take the R677 north and turn left at the first opportunity. Turn left again and follow the road, passing a crossroads and a church, for 4 kilometres. Drive up the farm track and ask at the farm for access. There are several standing stones on this land. This pair is to the north of the farm buildings.*

Whether these two standing stones constitute a stone pair is open to debate: there is only one stone marked on the Ordnance Survey map. The two stones stand 15 metres apart and are separated from each other by a field wall, but each can be seen from the other. The east stone is a lumpy conglomerate with many pebbles embedded in it. The west stone is 1.6 metres tall and smooth-sided with quartz veins running through it.

They stand on a gentle south-west-facing slope. The rising ground to the north-east blocks the view in that direction so that attention is drawn to the Monavullagh Mountains to the west. To the north the cairn-topped dome of Crauhaun Hill sits on the false horizon created by the rising slope.

Mini-Gazetteer – 7.5km NE there is a portal tomb at *Whitestown East*. 8.8km WNW there is a standing stone at *Carrigeen*. 10km WNW there is a standing stone at *Lyre*. 12km W there is a barrow at *Tooreen West*.

Ballinaclogh South
Standing Stone
OS Sheets 75 & 76: S 550 041

Directions: *From Tramore follow the R682 north for 4.5 kilometres. The last 2 kilometres of this route has no roads leading off it. Take a left turn that almost doubles back on the*

Above: The west stone from Ashtown stone pair.

Left: The west face of Ballinaclogh South standing stone.

main road. After 1.5 metres you come to a farm complex on the left. One hundred metres past the farmyard there is a field gate on the right from which the stone is visible.

This is a 2.2-metre-tall stone that appears to have been attacked at some point in the past. The top is very jagged, but a thin crust of lichen indicates that the damage is not recent. It stands a few metres from the edge of a field and can easily be seen from the field's gate.

Trees block the line of sight to a nearby rounded rock outcrop, which may have had some significance to the people that placed the stone here.

There are several interesting stones in the farmyard on the opposite side of the hedgerow next to the stone that may have originally been part of a monument in the area.

Mini-Gazetteer – 1.8km WNW there is a standing stone at **Ballymote**. 4.9km WSW there is a portal tomb at **Dunhill**. 7km NE there is a standing stone at **Ballindud**. 7.8km WSW there is a portal tomb at **Savagetown**.

Ballinadysert
Stone Pair
OS Sheet 75: S 358 200

Directions: From Carrick-on-Suir head west on the R680 towards Clonmel. After 3 kilometres the road bends to the left and then takes a sharp turn to the right. Turn left 100 metres after the sharp bend. Take the right fork after 800 metres and continue for 1.5 kilometres. Here you will find a farm track on the left. The stones are in a field to the right of this track, 300 metres along it.

There is every possibility that these two stones are actually the remains of a stone row that has been dismantled, as they stand over 15 metres apart. They are in a similar position to the six-stone row at **Rathmaiden**, on a broad plateau. Unlike the **Rathmaiden** example, these stones are not incorporated into a field boundary, but do have their view obscured by trees in all directions.

The tallest stone at the east end is 1.8 metres in height, while the other is slightly shorter. The former appears to have been worked and has relatively smooth sides compared to its companion.

Mini-Gazetteer – 6.1km E there is an ogham stone at **Crehanagh South**. 10km WNW there is a portal tomb at **Gurteen Lower**. 10.5km S there is a stone pair at **Ashtown**. 12.4km NNE there is a passage tomb at Knockroe (County Kilkenny).

Ballinadysert stone pair seen from the east.

Ballindud
Portal Tomb
OS Sheet: S 602 087

Directions: *From Waterford take the Tramore road south until you reach Ballindud roundabout. Turn left and then turn left again at the Couse Bridge roundabout. Fifty metres up this road you will be able to see a standing stone in the field to the left. Park here (carefully). From the gate walk straight along the edge of the field through the gap and into the next field. Turn left and walk around this field until you reach another gap. Pass through here and the tomb (or pile of brambles) can be seen to the left.*

Sadly, this monument has been left to the ravages of nature and is hidden beneath a thick covering of brambles and nettles. The remains are very simple and once resembled those of **Ballyquin** portal tomb 21 kilometres west, but with one extra stone standing at the rear of the capstone. In 1824, when Revd Ryland sketched this monument, the capstone is held aloft by two stones at the west end and rests on the floor at the other. Presumably, the capstone was originally supported at this end by the standing stone shown next to it. This raises questions about the original form of the Ballyquin monument.

Since then, the portal stones have both collapsed and are now lying recumbent below the capstone. With its heavy covering of vegetation, it is hard to tell if the stone

Ballindud portal tomb by R. Jacob from Revd Ryland's *History, Topography and Antiquities of the County and City of Waterford* (1824).

still stands near to the rear end of the capstone. Intensive farming in this field means that the plough comes to within 30 centimetres of the stones and no one takes care of the monument, making this one of the few neglected Waterford tombs.

Mini-Gazetteer – 3.6km SW there is a wedge tomb at ***Munmahoge***. 6.9km SW there is a ***Ballinaclogh South***. 13.1km NE there is a standing stone at Rochetown (County Kilkenny). 13.7km N there is a court tomb at Farnoge (County Kilkenny).

Ballindud
Standing Stone
OS Sheet 76: S 602 088

Directions: *From Waterford take the Tramore road south until you reach Ballindud roundabout. Turn left and then turn left again at the Couse Bridge roundabout. Fifty metres up this road you will be able to see the standing stone in the field to the left.*

This standing stone is not marked on the Ordnance Survey maps and the first time I saw it I thought it was the very disappointing remains of the portal tomb (also in ***Ballindud*** TD) 100 metres to the south.

Ballindud standing stone.

The stone is now in the middle of a large arable field, but is avoided by the farmer when he ploughs, leaving a small clearing around it. The stone is just 1.4 metres tall, which means that when the crops around it are at full height it can be difficult to see from the edge of the field.

Mini-Gazetteer – 4km SSW there is a passage tomb at ***Carriglong***. 6.7km WSW there is a portal tomb at ***Gaulstown***. 9.4km SW there is a passage tomb at ***Matthewstown***. 14.9km NE there is a stone row at Ballyfarnoge (County Kilkenny).

Ballingarry
Standing Stone
OS Sheets 75 & 82: S 459 013

Directions: *From Bunmahon take the R681 north towards Waterford. Take the second right turn, which is approximately 3.5 kilometres from Bunmahon. Continue for 800 metres and turn right at the first crossroads. The stone is visible from the road 200 metres south of the crossroads.*

The *Waterford Archaeological Inventory* lists it as 'leaning slightly to NNW', but it has now fallen over completely. It used to stand 1.6 metres tall.

Mini-Gazetteer – 4km ENE there is a portal tomb at ***Ballynageeragh***. 7.9km NE there is a stone pair at ***Raheens***. 10.8km NW there is a stone row at ***Rathmaiden***. 12.4km WSW there is a standing stone at ***Sheskin***.

Ballygunnertemple
Cists
OS Sheet 76: S 654 095

Directions: *Travel east out of Waterford on the R683 until you pass the turn-off for the R684. Four hundred metres after this junction you will come to a post office on the left. Opposite is a driveway leading up to a large house. The tomb is to the left of the drive about 30 metres from the road.*

When the Revd Ryland said that this monument, known as Mount Druid, was 'altogether too minute to deserve the appellation with which it has been dignified', he was not far wrong. There really is little to see here. All that remains are two parallel side-stones, a displaced lintel from one of the cists, and two perpendicular side-stones from the second. A mound next to them may be the soil that was removed when the cists were uncovered.

Mini-Gazetteer – 5.2km W there is a standing stone at **Ballindud**. 7.7km SW there is a passage tomb at **Carriglong**. 10.7km S there is a standing stone known as The White Wife at **Ballymacaw**. 13.2km W there is a standing stone at **Powersknock**.

Ballygunnertemple cist.

Ballyhussa
Standing Stone
OS Sheet 75: S 430 083

Directions: *From Kilmacthomas take the N25 east for around 3 kilometres and turn left. Turn right at the next crossroads and continue until you reach the next left turn. The stone could be seen in the field after this junction.*

Could be seen? When I revisited this fragile-looking stone in 2007 I could not see it, but it was definitely there in 2002. It was over 2 metres tall and just 15 centimetres thick. Its exposed position, in the centre of a field used for cattle, made this thin slab very vulnerable: perhaps the cows got through the electric fence that once protected the stone and rubbed a little too vigorously.

Mini-Gazetteer – 5.8km W there is a standing stone at ***Kealfoun***. 8.9km WSW there is an 'oghamised' stone pair at ***Garranmillon Lower***. 9.9km N there is a portal tomb at ***Ballyquin***. 13.7km ESE there is a wedge tomb at ***Carrickavrantry***.

Two views of Ballyhussa standing stone.

Ballymacaw – The White Lady
Standing Stone
OS Sheet 76: X 654 988

Directions: *An Ordnance Survey map is required in order to locate this site.*

The height of this stone is quite deceptive, because it stands in a small hollow. While approaching it appears to be quite short and its true height is only revealed when you are very close. It is actually just short of 2 metres tall.

Why the stone is called The White Lady is no longer known, but similar names are attached to standing stones elsewhere, e.g. The White Wife in Carnalridge TD, County Derry. The stone at Carnalridge was once whitewashed and had a small stone on top that was left unpainted, giving the impression of a lady in a white dress.[34]

The Ballymacaw stone has been cut so that it also looks like a head on broad shoulders. Was this stone once painted, hence its local name?

The White Lady's location is a thrilling one. It stands just metres from the top of high cliffs and the surf can clearly be heard crashing into them far below. There is a possibility that this stone was erected as a marker or beacon to direct sailors to the small cove 30 metres to the east of the stone. However, I think it is just too far back from the edge to have been seen from the sea.

Mini-Gazetteer – 5.6km NNE there is a passage tomb at *Harristown*. 8.8km NW there is a passage tomb at *Carriglong*. 11km NW there is a portal tomb at *Knockeen*. 13.6km WNW there is a portal tomb at *Gaulstown*.

Ballymote (Ballymoat)
Standing Stone
OS Sheets 75 & 76: S 533 048

Directions: *From Tramore take the R682 north. At the third crossroads turn left and continue for 2.5 kilometres until you come to a right turn. Take this and you will see the stone on your right after about 500 metres.*

This is Waterford's best-kept secret. At a height of 3.7 metres it is the tallest standing stone in the county. It also has a very aesthetic profile. One side of it is straight, while the other side bulges outwards near the base and then tapers to a round point. This shape is an uncanny echo of a stone in Cumbria, north England, at the stone circle known as Long Meg and Her Daughters. Sadly, unlike Long Meg, this one does not bear any rock art.

Ballymote standing stone from the north.

The stone stands on the top of a low ridge and can be seen very clearly from the main road to the south. Its association with a mound in the same field is uncertain.

Mini-Gazetteer – 16km NE there is a portal tomb at **Gaulstown**. 4.5km ENE there is a portal tomb at **Knockeen**. 8km ENE there is a standing stone at **Ballindud**. 14.3km E there is a passage tomb at **Harristown**.

Ballynageeragh
Portal Tomb
OS Sheets 75 & 82: S 495 030

Directions: *From Waterford take the N25 west and then the R681 south. Take the second left (after about 5 kilometres). Turn right at the junction after the crossroads (just before the church) and continue for 750 metres. You will come to a track on the right just before a left-hand bend with a little yellow dolmen sign opposite. Drive up this track until it widens out into a parking area of sorts. The dolmen is in the field ahead.*

Ballynageeragh portal tomb is part of Waterford's 'dolmen trail', a signposted route around the county taking in various prehistoric monuments. Over the years descriptions of this monument have varied in their interpretation. It is deemed complete and unique in form, as a portal tomb that never had portal stones.

Ballymacaw standing stone. The stick is one metre long.

Ballynageeragh portal tomb showing the modern wall to the right.

Ballynageeragh portal tomb from Du Noyer's 1860s report.

The capstone now rests upon the doorstone of the chamber and a modern concrete and brick wall erected by P. Murray & Sons in 1944. Early descriptions and plans show that the backstone of the chamber was in place in 1866.[35]

Prior to the erection of the concrete wall the site was excavated in 1940 by L. Mongey. Burnt bones, flint pebbles, a piece of poorly worked flint and charcoal from various trees (oak, hazel, alder, hawthorn and furze) were found in the chamber.[36] Beneath the rear of the capstone there is a smaller, secondary capstone giving the monument affinities to the portal tomb at *Knockeen*, which also has two capstones.

The axis of the 4-metre-long capstone is east-west, with the front facing westward. This is quite unusual for a portal tomb as they normally face east. However, the portal tomb at Knockeen also faces west.

Mini-Gazetteer – 4km WSW there is a standing stone at *Ballingary*. 7km NE there is a standing stone at *Whitfield North*. 8.8km ENE there is a wedge tomb at *Munmahoge*. 14.8km WNW there is a standing stone at *Ashtown*.

Ballynamona Lower
Court Tomb
OS Sheet 82: X 287 835

Directions: *From Dungarvan take the N25 towards Youghal and take the R674 towards Ringville. Take the second right-hand turn after about 3 kilometres. Follow this road for 5 kilometres and turn left at the fourth road. One and a half kilometres along this road turn left and then right after 300 metres. After 1 kilometre you will reach two gates – one across the road and one to the left. The tomb is 500 metres across the fields through the gate on the left.*

This is the most southerly of Ireland's court tombs. Only three of the stones that define the court are standing, but the 5-metre-long gallery is in good condition. This is divided into two chambers by a large orthostat that extends across three quarters of the gallery from the north wall. The walls are each formed by two slabs that lean against the dividing slab mentioned above and the small entrance jambs. A low sill stone between the entrance jambs defines the entrance. The wall slabs are placed directly onto the ground surface and supported by small packing stones. The gallery is divided into two sub-chambers, the rear of which is currently full of loose stones. The front chamber is clear (apart from the oddly placed information sign).

T.G.E. Powell[37] and his team excavated the site in 1938 under the Relief of Unemployment scheme. It was found that treasure seekers had plundered the monument in the fifty years prior to the excavation, but the finds were still interesting. Several sherds of pottery would have helped to date the structure, but these were found out of context; probably disturbed by the treasure seekers.

The gallery of Ballynamona court tomb with the sea beyond.

The floor of the court and first chamber was made from compacted clay. This appears to have been laid after the tomb had been built, because it did not go underneath the wall slabs. Stones from the cairn covered the floor area of the court. The rest of the cairn was present all around the monument, but the lack of a kerb meant that it was not possible to define its original extent.

The monument stands in a sad, rundown enclosure on a small cliff-top ridge overlooking two streams and the sea. To the south the views terminate at Mine Head, where you can see the lighthouse. To the east you can see along the Waterford coast for miles.

Mini-Gazetteer – 6.2km WNW there is a standing stone at **Ahaun**. 6.4km W there is a standing stone at **Monaneea**. 7.9km W there is a standing stone at **Glenwilliam**. 14km NNE there is a standing stone at **Sheskin**.

Ballyquin
Portal Tomb
OS Sheet 75: S 412 180

Directions: *From Carrick-on-Suir take the R676 south and then the R677. Two kilometres along the R677 turn right at Piquet's Crossroads (a five-way junction). After 1 kilometre turn right. A further one kilometre on and you will reach the bottom of a small valley. The tomb is in a field to the right of the road and is visible from here.*

Ballyquin portal tomb.

It is easy to believe that this delightful monument is in its original form, but the similar example at **Ballindud** indicates otherwise. It seems likely that the three stones forming the chamber were, at some time, taken away. Borlase mentions that:

> In the townland of Ballyquin, and Parish of Fenoagh, are two dolmens marked Cromlechs in Ord. Surv. Map No. 3.[38]

Only one survives today, but there is a standing stone in the same field as the portal tomb – perhaps this is all that remains of the second.

The existing tomb is built in the base of a valley so that it faces towards the slope of a hill that starts to rise 50 metres or so in front of it. The north-east end of the capstone is raised up on two portal stones, which are, unusually, set perpendicular to the axis of the tomb, leaving a small gap between them to form a doorway into the chamber. The west end now rests on the ground, but this is more likely due to the removal of the three stones that formed the chamber than its original design.

To the south-west of the tomb is a small stream and on the far side of that is a Holy Well.

Mini-Gazetteer – 7.1km NNE there is a portal tomb at Ballyhenebery (County Kilkenny). 9.3km SSW there is a stone row at **Rathmaiden**. 10.5km N there is a passage tomb on Bawnfree Hill (County Kilkenny). 14.6km SE there is a standing stone at **Powersknock**.

Ballyquin ogham stone. The stick is one metre long.

Ballyquin
Standing Stone/Ogham Stone
OS Sheet 75: S 421 188

Directions: *From Carrick-on-Suir take the R676 south and then the R677. Two kilometres along the R677 turn right at Piquet's Crossroads (a five-way junction). After approximately 400 metres there is a farm on the right. A short distance past the farm is a field gate on the same side of the road. The ogham stone stands by the southern gatepost inside the field.*

In *The Dolmens of Ireland* (1897) W.C. Borlase mentions a 12-foot-tall standing stone in the north of the townland, known as the Ballyquin High Stone. This is presumably that stone, but it is no longer 12 feet tall.

The stone now stands just inside a field gate. It was moved to this location from its original position in the middle of the field. Presumably, it lost some of its height when it was relocated: being set into the ground deeper than it was originally.

Sir Samuel Ferguson, former president of the Royal Irish Academy, reported the ogham inscription as reading:

CATABAR MOCO FIRIQORRB

However, he offers no interpretation or translation. Whereas, some thirty-two years later in 1909, Macalister read it as being:

CATABAR MOCOVIRICORB[39]

Fergusson went on to say of this stone:

> There are few more imposing monuments, or more like what we might be inclined to suppose survivals from Pagan times, in Ireland.[40]

I would not go quite that far, but it is one of the finest gateposts in Ireland! He elaborates that:

> Cromlechs exist near it, and a double-chambered cave, probably sepulchral.

One of the 'cromlechs' still exists (see *Ballyquin* portal tomb above), but the other two monuments are no longer to be seen. The double-chambered cave may have been a souterrain.

Mini-Gazetteer – 1.2km SW there is a portal tomb also in *Ballyquin* TD. 8.4km NNE there is a portal tomb at Owning (County Kilkenny). 9.7km NNE there is a standing stone at Garryduff (County Kilkenny). 14.8km SE there is a stone pair at *Raheens.*

Ballyquin
Standing Stone
OS Sheet 75: S 412 180

Directions*: From Carrick-on-Suir take the R676 south and then the R677. Two kilometres along the R677 turn right at Piquet's Crossroads (a five-way junction). After 1 kilometre turn right. A further 1 kilometre on you reach the bottom of a small valley. The standing stone and the tomb are in a field to the right of the road and visible from it.*

This 1.5-metre-tall standing stone is just 50 metres from the Ballyquin portal tomb (see previous page). It is most likely the remains of a second portal tomb marked on early Ordnance Survey maps.

Mini-Gazetteer – see *Ballyquin* portal tomb on previous page.

Ballyquin standing stone, with the portal tomb in the distance.

The fallen stone at Boherboy.

Boherboy
Standing Stone
OS Sheet 82: X 202 842

Directions: *Head north from Ardmore on the R673. Turn left onto the N25 and drive south for 300 metres. This stone lies in a field to the west of the N25 and can be seen from a stone-built gateway.*

In 2003 this stone was still standing, but has since fallen. It now lies where it once stood, on the top of a wide plateau 100 metres from a main road. The ground around the base of the stone is well trodden, presumably by cattle using the stone as a rubbing post. The *Waterford Archaeological Inventory* noted that it stood 2.2 metres tall, but was not set firmly into the ground and this localised erosion could have been the reason that the stone fell.

Mini-Gazetteer – 1.7km there is a standing stone at *Glenwilliam*. 2.8km ENE there is a standing stone at *Ahaun*. 5.5km E there is a standing stone at *Lagnagoushee*. 8.6km E there is a court tomb at *Ballynamona Lower*.

Carrickavrantry
Wedge Tomb
OS Sheets 75 & 76: S 551 018

Directions: *This site is not easy to find. From Tramore take the R682 north-west and then the first left. About 400 metres after the second right-hand turn you will come to a track on the right. Park here and follow the track and then the sunken path around the fields. The tomb is situated in the corner of the field to the right, next to the path, where it takes a sharp-right turn.*

The structural remains of this monument are still embedded in its mound. One end of the gallery has been uncovered and the end stone and one capstone have been removed, allowing access.

The gallery is 2 metres long, 1 metre wide and 70 centimetres high. It is aligned north-east to south-west and is open at the south-west. The remaining capstone is a split boulder with its smooth side forming the chamber's ceiling. The orthostat forming the south side of the gallery is damaged and a small stone fills a gap in its top. Whether this is an original feature or the result of attempts to break into the tomb is unknown.

The location overlooks Carrickavrantry Lough to the west, which is just visible across the fields, through the hedgerows and trees that stand between them. To the north there are many rocky outcrops that create wonderful shapes on the horizon.

Carrickavrantry wedge tomb, looking north-east.

The spelling of Carrickavrantry appears in several forms including Carrickavantry and Carrigavantry. Its name originally meant 'the rock of the quernstone maker'.[41]

Mini-Gazetteer – 2.3km N there is a standing stone at **Ballinaclogh South**. 2.5km WNW there is a passage tomb at **Matthewstown**. 4.5km NNW there is a portal tomb at **Gaulstown**. 12.7km E there is a passage tomb at **Harristown**.

Carrigeen
Standing Stone
OS Sheet 75: S 281 127

Directions: *From Clonmel take the R678 east towards Rathgormack. Take the second right-hand turn after passing Clonmel Golf Club. Continue for 8 kilometres until you reach a T-junction. Turn left and follow the road and turn left just after crossing Birchell's Bridge. This is a cul-de-sac and leads to a car park. Once parked, walk up the road and you will see the standing stone ahead of you.*

There are few standing stones as well placed as this one. It stands high on a north-west-facing slope at the head of the long, deep valley formed by the River Suir. At 2.5 metres tall it is quite imposing, but its location means that it cannot be seen against the sky as you walk up to it. Its profile is irregular and tapers to a very fine point, making it look like an oversized stone dagger.

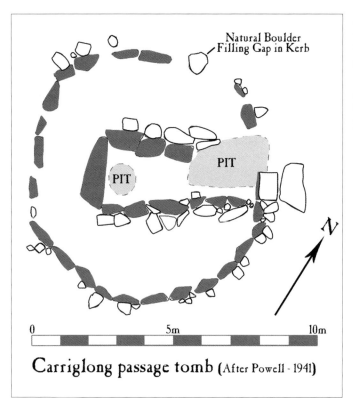

Above: Looking west past Carrigeen standing stone.

Left: Plan of Carriglong passage tomb.

Natural Boulder Filling Gap in Kerb

PIT

PIT

N

0   5m   10m

Carriglong passage tomb (After Powell - 1941)

The location is very near to an ancient route over the Monavullagh Mountains, called The Gap, which is popular with walkers today.

On a small plateau below the stone there is a large burnt mound or *fulacht fia*.

Mini-Gazetteer – 3.4km WSW there is a stone circle at **Tooreen**. 8.7km ESE there is a standing stone at **Ashtown**. 9.7km SW there is a stone row at **Knockboy**. 12.1km S there is a cairn at **Crohaun**.

Carriglong
Passage Tomb
OS Sheets 75 & 76: S 951 050

Directions: *Head south on the N25 from Waterford and take the first left after passing the R686 junction. Take the second left and continue for about 1 kilometre until you reach a small garden centre. The tomb is in the field to the rear of this.*

In 1939 T.G.E. Powell excavated[42] this passage tomb, while J. Hawkes excavated **Harristown** in the same year. The findings were quite surprising, especially the dating evidence that placed its construction in the Bronze Age.

Like **Harristown**, the monument is constructed on a bed of clay, which was covered in parts by a spread of charcoal. This was concentrated in the southwest quadrant between the passage orthostats and the kerb. Signs of burning on the inner face of two kerbstones and some of the stones supporting the passages orthostats showed that the burning took place after the tomb was built, but before the cairn was thrown up over it.

Unlike Harristown, the construction quality was not very high. The orthostats forming the passage and chamber at Carriglong were set only shallowly into the clay floor. None of the twenty-two kerbstones were visible before excavation. Most of these were found *in situ*, but six had become displaced. The sockets for these stones were easy to identify and the fallen stones were replaced. The kerbstones were set into shallow sockets 'pointy-end' down, making them top-heavy. To help keep them upright the sockets were packed with small pebbles and soil, and each kerbstone had stones placed against their outer faces. These supporting stones were mainly resting on the old ground surface, but some were set. An interruption in the kerb was noted to one side of the entrance. No sockets for missing stones were identified in this gap, but there is a natural boulder in the middle of it.

The 5.5-metre-long passage has five stones along the south side and three on the north. Treasure seekers had removed two stones from the north side when they dug one of the two pits inside the passage and chamber. At the entrance the passage is 1 metre wide, expanding to 2 metres at the rear (south-west). A low, smooth-sided stone partially blocks the entrance.

The pits dug by the tomb raiders caused a lot of damage inside the passage. All that remained were two cremation deposits. One of these was associated with two small flint scrapers and some small pottery sherds, while the other was near to a rough flint pebble. A total of eighteen pottery sherds were found, but all of these were too small to reconstruct the shapes of the pots they came from. Due to the small size of the flint scrapers, Powell suggested that these were made specifically to be buried, but at the time of the dig microliths (very small stone tools) were not a recognised type. A round beach pebble found amongst the cairn material showed signs that it had been used as a hammer stone.

Such was the difference between the findings here compared to any other tomb excavated in Ireland, Powell finished the conclusion of his report with the following:

> The discovery of another megalithic culture in County Waterford, one of direct continental origin, unlike that represented by the segmented Gallery Grave at Ballynamona, or the Portal Chambers such as Knockeen, emphasises the importance of this coast-line which could offer so many agreeable landing places to the sea-farers of Atlantic Europe.[43]

It is interesting to note that the site is located on a significant slope, but no attempt was made to strengthen the tomb on the down-slope side. The wedge tomb at Baurnadomeeny (County Tipperary) was similarly built on a slope and significant effort was made to make the lower side of the structure secure against slippage.[44]

Powell notes that no local folklore about the site exists apart from that the tomb was the grave of a hero or warrior and a nearby rocky outcrop was thought to be the grave of his wife. In a recent publication, Andy Taylor expands on this to say that the tomb is said to be the grave of a local giant called Longa, who had a long-running feud with his brother, Conan of Drumcannon.[45]

Mini-Gazetteer – 4.2km WSW there is a standing stone at *Ballinaclogh South*. 6.5km WSW there is a passage tomb at *Matthewstown*. 8.8km SE there is a standing stone at *Ballymacaw*. 14.5km NNE there is a bullaun stone at Atateemore (County Kilkenny).

Castlereagh 1
Ring Barrow
OS Sheet 75: S 212 103

Directions: *From Dungarvan take the R672 north towards Clonmel. Cross the N72 and continue along the R672. After 5 kilometres the road turns sharply right and then right again. Continue for 6 kilometres to the second crossroads and turn right. Take the first left and travel another 4.5 kilometres. This road is very straight, so if you reach a right-hand*

The southern Castlereagh ring barrow, looking west.

bend you have gone too far. Towards the end of this road you pass pine plantations on either side of the road. The barrow is in a field to the left of the road, 300 metres after the plantations, and can be seen from the gate.

The low bank of this barrow has been disturbed, but its form is still visible. It is 10 metres in diameter and the surrounding bank is 50 centimetres high. A field hedge runs across its northern edge.

It is located on the western foothills of Milk Hill, which rises high to the east of the site. Slightly higher ground to the south blocks the views in that direction, so the observer is forced to look westwards towards the Knockmealdown Mountains and the Galtees beyond those.

Mini-Gazetteer – 4km ENE there is a stone circle at ***Tooreen***. 5.1km S there is a stone row at ***Knockboy***. 7.6km SE there is a cairn at ***Scartnadrinnymountain***. 12.1km WSW there is a cairn at ***Glennafallia***.

Castlereagh 2
Ring Barrow
OS Sheet 75: S 212 104

Directions: *This barrow is in the next field to the north from Castlereagh 1 above.*

This barrow is in much better condition than its partner in the field to the south. It is isolated in the centre of the field and so is undisturbed by hedgerows. The

The northern Castlereagh ring barrow, looking south-west.

1-metre-tall bank that defines the site is complete and where it is slightly worn it is possible to see that it is packed with small pebbles. This extra ballast in its construction has probably helped preserve its form. In the centre there is a low-raised area separated from the bank by a shallow fosse.

The views are exactly the same as those from **Castlereagh 1** above.

Coolnasmearmountain
Standing Stone
OS Sheets 75 & 82: S 258 008

Directions: *A GPS and map are required in order to find this monument.*

This is a short, stocky standing stone that is as wide as it is tall. At just over 1 metre tall it is not particularly imposing, but its location more than makes up for that. The stone stands on a very gentle, south-facing slope and offers wonderfully peaceful views.

A smaller stone stands 10 centimetres from its north face and may be a fragment of the larger stone that has been sheered off, but the shapes of the two do not match. This second stone is a bit of a mystery.

Mini-Gazetteer – 1.9km NE there is a standing stone at **Treenearla Commons**. 3km N there is an archaeological complex at **Coumaraglinmountain**. 6.2km NNE there is a cairn at **Cutteen North**. 11.7km N there is a standing stone at **Lyre**.

Coolnasmearaghmountain standing stone from the east.

Capstone of cist in Coumaraglinmountain (1) cairn.

Coumaraglinmountain 1
Cairn
OS Sheets 75 & 82: S 268 044

Directions: *This monument requires a GPS and an Ordnance Survey map to find.*

This is one of the larger cairns in this very monumentally busy townland. It is 20 metres in diameter and at least 2 metres high. The top of the monument has been robbed, exposing a big ruined cist at the centre. This chamber is 2 metres by 1 metre in plan, which is larger than average.

Thirty metres west of the cairn there is a pointed standing stone. A line from the centre of the cairn through this stone extends towards the Knockmealdown Mountains, where several V-shaped notches could mark significant sunsets. The majority of the monuments in this complex have features that favour the west, and the site's location, at the base of a steep west-facing slope, also points to the westerly aspect being very important to the builders.

Mini-Gazetteer – 1.5km NNW there is a cairn at **Cutteen North**. 6km W there is a stone row at **Knockboy**. 8.8km N there is a stone pair at **Knockanaffrin**. 12.6km W there is a standing stone at **Mweeling**.

Coumaraglinmountain 2
Cairn
OS Sheets 75 & 82: S 268 043

Directions: *This monument requires a GPS and an Ordnance Survey map to find.*

The remains of this cairn are not much higher than the surrounding peat level, but they are quite extensive. There are two cists set within the cairn, one of which is completely open while the other is still partially closed by its capstone.

Like the cairn next to it (see previous page), this cairn has an associated standing stone to the west of it. This cairn's stone is a little further away than that of the other cairn; once again the strong tendency towards westerly alignments is present.

Coumaraglinmountain 3
Henge/Barrow
OS Sheets 75 & 82: S 261 035

Directions: *A GPS and an Ordnance Survey map are required to find this monument.*

Partially open cist in Coumeraglin Mountain (2) cairn.

Coumeraglin Mountain barrow/henge sky-lined, seen approaching from the north

Coumeraglin Mountain (4)/ Cutteen South standing stones from the south.

This monument is marked on the Ordnance Survey map as a barrow and it could well be a large ring barrow. However, there is a well-defined inner ditch and there are two openings in the bank. This could make it a small henge.

The bank is 1 metre high and 15 metres in diameter. It is situated at the top of a slope overlooking a stone circle, several standing stones and a cairn field. This location gives the site splendid views to the north, west and south. Easterly views are blocked by Farbreaga Mountain, which rises steeply just 500 metres to the east of the site.

Coumaraglinmountain 4 (Cutteen South)
Standing Stone
OS Sheets 75 & 82: S 279 054

Directions: *This stone stands in the Bearna na Madra gap in the Monavullagh Mountains and requires an Ordnance Survey map to find.*

There are few standing stones in Ireland that require as much effort to reach as this fine 2-metre-tall specimen. It stands in the saddle between Farbreaga Mountain and Seefin Mountain at a height of 500 metres above sea level. It is also on the boundary between Cutteen South and Coumaraglinmountain TDs. The nearest approachable road is at 250 metres and the slopes in between are very steep.

The 1.3-metre-wide stone is set so that its axis runs east-west. This means that when viewed from below its narrow side is edge on. Even so, it is still visible from over 2 kilometres away. The southern face of the stone has been whitewashed and, judging by the paint's condition in this exposed position, this practice seems to have been continued until quite recently.

Coumaraglinmountain 5
Standing Stone
OS Sheets 75 & 82: S 260 038

Directions: *This monument requires a GPS and an Ordnance Survey map to find.*

Standing alongside the track that leads to the *Coumaraglinmountain* complexes, this standing stone is the first monument you encounter here. It can be quite easy to miss it though because your attention is torn between negotiating the rough track and staring at the beauty of the mountains in front of you.

This is a rough stone about 1.6 metres tall. Its long axis is oriented along the track on an east-west line. To the north the Araglin River Valley rises up, with its eastern side formed by Seefin Mountain and *Scartnadrinnymountain* on its west.

Coumaraglinmountain (5) standing stone, looking east towards the main complexes.

Coumaraglinmountain (6) stone circle, looking towards Scartnadrinny Mountain and the Knockmealdown Mountains beyond.

To the south of the stone there is a low round-topped hill that has some very denuded cairns on its summit.

Near to the stone, just at the base of the round hill to its south, there is a white *Fogra* protection sign hiding in the bracken, but visible from the track. This is next to some low piles of stones. These are hut sites, possibly the homes of the people that built the complexes above.

Coumaraglinmountain 6
Stone Circle
OS Sheets 75 & 82: S 269 048

Directions: *This site requires a GPS to find.*

This stone circle is part of the vast complex of monuments on the south-western slopes of Seefin Mountain, below the Bearna na Madra gap. It is 3.5 metres in diameter and the heights of the stones vary from just 20 centimetres above the peat level to over 1 metre. The tallest stones are on the west side, facing towards the Knockmealdown Mountains.

Coumaraglinmountain 7
Stone Circle
S 261 035

Directions: *This site requires a GPS to find.*

Like the stone circle 1.5 kilometres to the north this is a small circle. It is circa 4 metres in diameter with stones not much taller than 50 centimetres above the peat level. Many of the stones are either missing or buried beneath the peat. There is one arc of six tightly packed stones at the west part of its circumference. Opposite these just two stones can be seen.

Coumaraglinmountain (7) stone circle, looking towards Scartnadrinny Mountain.

Roughly 15 metres to the north-west there is a small standing stone: a 50-centimetre-tall outlier that points towards the nearby bulbous rocky outcrop on *Scartnadrinnymountain*.

Mini-Gazetteer – 1.9km SE there is a cairn at **Treenearla Commons**. 3.2km SSE there is a cairn at **Crohaun**. 8.2km N there is a stone circle at **Tooreen**. 9.1km E there is an 'oghamised' stone pair at **Garranmillon Lower**. 10.8km WNW there is a stone pair at Aughavanlomaun (County Cork).

Crehanagh South
Standing Stone/Ogham Stone
OS Sheet 75: S 419 197

Directions: *From Carrick-on-Suir follow the signs for Kilmacthomas. Nine hundred metres after the junction between the R677 and R676 take a farm track on the left. Go up this rough track to the farm buildings. The ogham stone can be seen in a field to the right, two gates beyond these buildings.*

Waterford has several 'oghamised' standing stones, such as the one in **Ballyquin** TD. This is another example. It is 2 metres tall and bears inscriptions down two adjacent edges on its south side. Today, the inscription is all but illegible, but in 1909 Macalister read it as being:

VOCAGNI MAQI CUR(I)T[46]

Crehanagh South standing stone, showing part of the ogham inscription.

The top of the stone appears damaged. This could be the result of weathering and frost action, or, as is suggested in the *Waterford Archaeological Inventory*, a deliberate attempt to destroy the stone prior to its inscription.

The stone's profile is very irregular, but it is essentially rectangular in cross section. Its profile is quite similar to that of the impressive standing stone in **Ballymote** TD, but on a smaller scale.

To the north of its location is a high, bare rock-strewn hill that dominates the south-facing plateau on which the stone stands. To the west, the dark outline of the Monavullagh and Comeragh Mountains forms the horizon, with the stone's axis pointing in the direction of their southern extent.

Mini–Gazetteer – 1.7km SSW there is a standing stone at **Ballyquin**. 5.8km S there is a portal tomb at **Whitestown East**. 11.5km SSW there is a stone pair at **Ashtown**. 12.5km N there is a standing stone at Kiltrassy (County Kilkenny).

Croagh
Stone Pair
OS Sheets 75 & 82: S 509 036

Directions: *Although this site is very close to Dunhill, directions are not easy to give, so an Ordnance Survey map is required to find these stones. However, note that the track on the OS map has moved to the other side of the stones, which can now be found 10 metres from a sharp left-hand bend.*

The taller of the Croagh stone pair.

Sadly, these two stones are now hidden beneath ivy and trees, and behind high brambles and bracken. The shorter of the two stones is 2 metres tall, while the other is over 3 metres tall. When standing in front of them, however, neither appear to be this tall as they are incorporated into a drystone wall.

The shorter stone is directly behind a thorn tree, making it very difficult to spot, especially when covered in ivy. The taller stone is often cleared of ivy, but this soon grows back. These obstacles and the row of pine trees that towers over the stones completely block out the views from this site.

Mini-Gazetteer – 1.5km WSW there is a portal tomb at *Ballynegeeragh*. 5.7km NNE there is a standing stone at *Whitfield North*. 10.6km ENE there is a portal tomb at *Ballindud*. 14.4km W are the *Drumlohan* ogham stones.

Crohaun
Cairn
OS Sheets 75 & 82: S 275 006

Directions: *From Lemybrien follow the N25 south for 1.5 kilometres and turn right at Downey's Crossroads. At the next T-junction turn left and then left again at the next. A little over 1 kilometre along this road turn right onto the pass road. After 3.5 kilometres there is a parking area on the left. Continue past this for 800 metres until you reach a lane to the left that heads south towards some radio masts on the top of Crohaun Hill. This track*

The cairn on the top of Crohaun Mountain, as seen from the north-west.

is very rutted, so I suggest parking at the road and walking the rest of the way. When you reach the gate across the track, turn left, up the hill, to walk up to the cairn.

In 1987 a huge concrete cross was erected on top of this well-placed cairn, making it even more conspicuous in the landscape. The cross is bright white and even the Ordnance Survey trig point has received a coat of bright blue paint.

The cairn itself is substantial. It is 30 metres in diameter and over 3 metres high, making it one of Waterford's largest cairns. There are no visible traces of a kerb, but its hilltop position indicates that it may be a passage tomb.

Crohaun is an isolated hill at the southern end of the Monavullagh Mountains, separated from them by The Pass – an ancient route through the mountains. As would be expected from such a position, the views are fantastic and these alone make the climb worthwhile; to the south you can see Dungarvan and the craggy coastline; to the north the Monavullagh Mountains, and to the north-west the spectacular Knockmealdown Mountains. In the valley to the north, on the other side of the mountain pass road, there are several other cairns and a fine standing stone in *Treenearla Commons* TD.

It's interesting to note that the cairn can not be seen from the bottom of the Maum Pass to the north. It seems to have been situated with a view to it being a prominent feature when seen from the flat lands to the west of the mountains.

Mini-Gazetteer – 1.3km N there is a cairn at *Treenearla Commons*. 8.3km ESE there is a standing stone at *Sheskin*. 11.5km NNW there is a stone row at *Tooreen West*. 13.6km N there is a stone circle at *Knockanaffrin*.

Crohaun
Cairn
OS Sheets 75 & 82: S 276 018

Directions: *From Lemybrien follow the N25 south for 1.5 kilometres and turn right at Downey's Crossroads. At the next T-junction turn left and then left again at the next. A little over 1 kilometre along this road turn right onto the pass road. After 3.5 kilometres there is a parking area on the left. Park here and walk up the road to the next field gate. The cairn can just be seen from this gate, 50 metres to the south-west.*

Only 30 centimetres of this cairn is visible above the peat, making it very difficult to size properly. It is located in a position that feels like the valley bottom, but the site is still quite high up. This is the Maum Pass and the Dalligan Valley descends from here.

With Farbreaga Mountain to the north and Crohaun Mountain to the south this is a very closed-in location, but the views to the south-east open out as far as the coast.

Looking over the cairn in the Maum Pass and down the Dalligan Valley.

Mini-Gazetteer – 500m W there is a standing stone at ***Treenearla Commons***. 4km NW there is a stone pair at ***Kilbrien Lower***. 5km N there is a cairn at ***Cutteen North***. 10.9km N there is a standing stone at ***Carrigeen***.

Crohaun
Standing Stone
OS Sheets 75 & 82: S 274 016

Directions: *This stone is hidden in amongst many boulders and requires a GPS to locate. It is not marked on the Ordnance Survey maps.*

To the south of the pass road, south of the Monavullagh Mountains, the fields are littered with rocks and boulders. Several raised areas could be peat-covered cairns. Amongst the boulders there are a number of stones that could be unrecorded standing stones – this is the most prominent of these.

At just over 1 metre tall and leaning at a 60-degree angle, it is not particularly impressive, but its proximity to so many monuments in this valley make it part of an extensive megalithic complex: within 500 metres there are four cairns and a selection of standing stones, such as the one in ***Treenearla Commons*** TD.

Mini-Gazetteer – 6.6km WNW there is a stone row at ***Knockboy***. 8.2km ENE there is a stone pair at ***Garranmillon Lower***. 11.3km NE there is a standing stone at ***Ashtown***. 12.6km N there is a stone pair at ***Knockanaffrin***.

Crohaun standing stone.

Cutteen North
Cairn
OS Sheet 75: S 275 068

Directions: *This site requires an Ordnance Survey map, a GPS and stout boots to find. It is best approached from the west via the Bearna na Madra Gap*

From below, you can see a large bump on the top of Seefin Mountain, which you assume is the cairn. This bump is actually a rocky outcrop – the cairn is 50 metres to the south of this and too low to be seen from the lowlands around the hill.

The cairn has been severely disturbed. The centre has been hollowed out to provide shelter for walkers, but this has revealed a possible stone-lined cist. The depth of this excavation implies that the peat on top of the mountain is very deep, maybe up to 2 metres in places. Considering this, the cairn may have been visible from below when it was first constructed.

Mini-Gazetteer – 5km S there is a standing stone at **Treenearla Commons**. 5.5km NNW there is a stone circle at **Tooreen**. 5.8km WSW there is a stone row at **Knockboy**. 9.5km NNE there is a standing stone at **Graigavalla**.

Cutteen South
Cairn
OS Sheet 75: S 279 061

Directions: *see Cutteen North on previous page.*

Cutteen North cairn.

This small, ruined cairn is positioned so that it can be seen only from the eastern side of the Monavullagh Mountains. Sadly, its robbed-out state means that even from the west it is now very difficult to see from below.

The remains are 5 metres in diameter and no more than 50 centimetres high. The views from this vantage point are great. Below the monument to the south is the Bearna na Madra gap, a saddle between Seefin and Farbreaga Mountains. At the base of the slopes to the west of the hill are the **Coumaraglinmountain** complexes. To the north Seefin Mountain continues to rise, while to the east the mountains continue for a while before giving way to the plains beyond.

Mini-Gazetteer – 4.1km S there is a cairn at **Treenearla Commons**. 5.5km S there is a cairn at **Crohaun**. 6.6km N there is a standing stone at **Carrigeen**. 9.3km ENE there is a standing stone at **Kilclooney**.

Drumlohan
Ogham Stones
OS Sheets 75 & 82: S 367 013

Directions: *Take the R677 and then the N25 south from Kilmacthomas and take the first road on the left. Continue for 2 kilometres past the first crossroads. There is a track on the left. Follow this track and it will bring you to the stones.*

When the banks of a rath were cleared away in the 1800s a souterrain was uncovered. Its layout was nothing special, just a single rectangular chamber, but its structure incorporated many ogham stones. These were used as roof lintels and as parts of the walls.

Cutteen South cairn.

Within the chamber ogham stones are built into both walls. The inscribed stones from the roof now stand around the outside of the open souterrain. The complete inscriptions read:

BIGU MAQI LAG
BIR MAQI MUCOI ROTTAIS
& MANU MAGUNO GATI MOCOI MOCORBO

A wooden fence erected around the site has, over recent years, deteriorated badly and shows that the site is no longer cared for the way it once was.

Mini-Gazetteer – 3.2km NNW there is a stone pair at **Garranmillon Lower**. 9.2km E there is a standing stone at **Ballingary**. 10km WNW there is a cairn at **Cutteen South**. 10.8km E there is a portal tomb at **Savagetown**.

Dunhill
Portal Tomb
OS Sheets 75 & 82: S 505 021

Directions: *From Waterford take the N25 west and then the R681 south. Take the second left (after about 5 kilometres). Continue for about 3.5 kilometres until you pass a church on your right. Four hundred metres after the church, on the left by a barn, you will find this tomb.*

Drumlohan souterrain and assembled ogham stones.

Drumlohan ogham stones.

In recent years, trees have been planted in front of this monument, almost obscuring it from the road. It is still possible to see it a short way along the road from the nearby farmyard, but this is not its best angle. Actually, to be fair, this ruinous portal tomb does not really have a best angle.

The large, bulbous capstone rests on one orthostat and some rubble. It is impossible to say whether the remaining upright stone was one of the portal stones or from the chamber section. If it was a portal stone then the original monument was not a large one.

Mini-Gazetteer – 1.3km NW there is a portal tomb at **Ballynageeragh**. 5km N there is a stone pair at **Raheens**. 9.1km ENE there is a passage tomb at **Carriglong**. 14.4km WNW there is a standing stone at **Kealfoun**.

Dyrick
Standing Stone
OS Sheets 74 & 82: S 153 047

Directions: *From Dungarvan follow the signs for Lismore along the R672 and then the N72. Six and a half kilometres along the N72 turn right onto the R671 in the direction of Clonmel. Five kilometres on you will go around a hairpin bend. Turn left at the next opportunity. Following this road will bring you to Dyrick Hill. Continue past the hill until you come to a sharp right-hand bend. This standing stone is through a gateway to the left of the road on the bend.*

This is the most interesting standing stone in a group concentrated around Dyrick Hill, a prominent, but small, round hill at the eastern edge of the Knockmealdown Mountains. It has the most unusual form: looking like an art nouveau skyscraper.

Sadly, the pine plantation that surrounds it on three sides obscures its views of Dyrick Hill. At 2 metres tall it would be quite imposing if it was left to stand in an open field.

Mini-Gazetteer – 1km N there is a standing stone at **Mweeling**. 10.9km E there is a stone circle at **Coumaraglinmountain**. 11.4km NE there is a barrow at **Tooreen West**. 13.9km NE there is a standing stone at **Lyre**.

Garranmillon Lower
Stone Pair/Ogham Stones
OS Sheets 75 & 82: S 352 041

Directions: *From Kilmacthomas take the N25 south towards Lemybrien. Five hundred metres past the second turning on the right after the R677, there is a farm track on the right-*

Dunhill portal tomb.

Dyrick standing stone.

hand side of the road. Two hundred metres past this there is another track that leads to a
new bungalow. Ask here for access to the stones.

It is very unusual to find a stone pair where both stones bear an ogham
inscription. It is so unusual that you might think they are two ogham stones
that have been brought together from separate locations, but these do (at first
sight) appear to belong together. However, an account of the stones from 1896
tells all:

> On the north-eastern brow of an eminence in that townland one Ogham Stone
> stands, and another lies a few yards north of a killeen that has been enclosed by the
> present proprietor of the land. Evidently the now disused burial place included at
> one time the site of the Ogham Stones, which are Pagan mortuary monuments, and
> was a Pagan cemetery [*sic*] ('ferta') before it became a Christian place of sepulture,
> ('reilic') on the erection of a diminutive Church, ('cillin') whose foundations still
> are there.

> Neither Mr. Richard R. Brash's 'Ogham-inscribed Monuments of the Gaedhil', nor
> Sir Samuel Ferguson's 'Ogham Inscriptions in Ireland, Wales, and Scotland' mentions
> these Stones. Apparently, the first account of them in print is that by the Revd Canon
> Hewson in the *Journal of the Royal Society of Antiquarians of Ireland*, March, 1896, as fol-
> lows:– 'Close outside the Killeen is a tall pillar stone over seven feet high. It bears an
> Ogham inscription very much worn by weather and the rubbing of cattle, and long
> known to antiquarians; for which reason I shall not further mention it. My business
> is with a big boulder lying on its side, about five yards distant. This boulder measures
> 8 feet 2 inches in length, varies from 33 to 12 inches in width, and is of a nearly uni-
> form depth of 13 or 14 inches. It was sunk in the ground by its own weight, but Miss
> Fairholme of Comeragh had it turned over in my presence by a number of navvies;
> and then there appeared a faint Ogham inscription. It appeared uninjured, except by
> the uniform wear of the weather during the time it had stood upright, and seems to
> have consisted originally of a single word ... MELAGI or MELANGI ...'[47]

Both stones are around 2 metres tall and stand 2 metres apart on an east–west
axis. The ogham inscriptions are carved onto the west edge of each stone. The
western stone has the clearest inscription, but this is still unreadable today. In 1945
Macalister read it as:

GOSOCTAS MUCOI CORBI

He read the other stone to be:

MELAGIA[48]

Garranmillon Lower 'oghamised' stone pair, with The Monavullagh Mountains beyond.

Twenty metres to the south of the stones there is a rectangular enclosure, which is the site of a long-gone church.

Mini-Gazetteer – 5km N there is a standing stone at **Ashtown**. 8.5km WSW there is a cairn at **Crohaun**. 11.1km ESE there is a standing stone at **Ballingary**. 12.3km E there is a portal tomb at **Savagetown**.

Gaulstown
Kist
OS Sheets 75 & 76: S 540 062

Directions: *From Waterford take the N25 west. Turn south along the R682 towards Tramore. Turn right at the second crossroads and continue for 1.5 kilometres. Shortly after a right-hand bend you will see a farm track on the left. Park beyond the gate and walk up the track for 200 metres, where you will find a kissing gate on the left. The kist is just inside this.*

Just inside the entrance to the small enclosure that houses **Gaulstown** portal tomb (see below) there is a small megalithic kist. The capstone is 2 metres long by 1 metre deep. This may have been incorporated in the long cairn of the portal tomb (if it ever had one).

Gaulstown megalithic kist.

Gaulstown
Portal Tomb
OS Sheets 75 & 76: S 540 062

Directions: *From Waterford take the N25 west. Turn south along the R682 towards Tramore. Turn right at the second crossroads and continue for 1.5 kilometres. Shortly after a right-hand bend you will see a farm track on the left. Park beyond the gate and walk up the track for 200 metres, where you will find a kissing gate on the left. The tomb is through this.*

Hidden in a small clearing in a clump of trees 100 metres along a small track the structural beauty of this monument comes as a surprise when you first see it. The 4.2-metre-long capstone is held 2.5 metres above the ground by two fine portal stones and a backstone that slopes inwards slightly. Inside the chamber there is a concrete construction and the bases of the orthostats are also firmly cemented. This is a good example of unsympathetic reconstruction/preservation.

The structure of the monument seems complete. Instead of a high doorstone there is a low sillstone. The entrance faces south-east towards the nearby rocky slopes of Carrick-a-Roirk Hill (the Rock of the Prospect). If a straight line were projected in this direction it would pass very close to the portal tomb in **Knockeen** TD.

The *Waterford Archaeological Inventory* describes the monument as 'In scrub at the bottom of a steep N-facing slope ...'[49] and drawings from the 1800s show it in the open. Now, trees tightly surround the site, giving it a claustrophobic feel

Gaulstown portal tomb.

at times and blocking out all its views, which would take in the Monavullagh Mountains to the west. At certain times of the year it is almost impossible to see the monument, as it becomes smothered in tall bracken. It would be great if the site was opened up once more.

Just inside the entrance to the enclosure, on the right, is a large slab. This is the capstone of a megalithic kist. It was presumably a later insertion into the portal tomb's cairn.

Mini-Gazetteer – 3.5km E there is a portal tomb at **Knockeen**. 9.5km WSW there is a standing stone at **Ballingary**. 11.2km W there is a standing stone at **Ballyhussa**. 13.8km E there is a passage tomb at **Harristown**.

Glennafallia
Cairn
OS Sheet: S 094 075

Directions: *An Ordnance Survey map is recommended for this monument. From Cappoquin, head north on the R669 towards Clogheen for 4.5 kilometres. Turn right where Mount Mellory Monastery is signposted. Continue on this road, past Mt. Mellory, for 6.5 kilometres. Shortly after you pass into County Tipperary you will find a parking spot on the left-hand side of the road. From here a track leads up the side of Knockmeal Mountain.*

Walk up this and then head south above the forestry plantation. This track will lead you to the base of Knocknafallia. From here it is a very steep climb to the top.

This cairn is unique to Waterford, if not to the whole of Ireland. With a 10-metre diameter it is quite small, but its features make it special. Several of its kerbstones are still visible, protruding through the disturbed stones that have slid down from the upper part of the cairn. These kerbstones are arranged so that they alternate between being set around the circumference and at right angles to it. This feature is easiest to see around the north side.

On the north-western side of the cairn there is a 1-metre-tall standing stone that leans slightly to the west. The upper surface of this stone is parallel to the ground, so it is possible that the stone always leant in this manner. There is a spread of large quartz stones scattered about its base.

On the opposite side of the cairn, facing south-east, there is an open-fronted kist – a single roof-stone resting on two side-stones with a drystone rear wall. This chamber is about 1 metre across, 50 centimetres deep and 50 centimetres tall, although its floor is full of cairn material. There are many small quartz pebbles mixed in amongst the rubble in and around it. The opening faces towards the Monavullagh Mountains, the most prominent feature of which, from here, is the most southerly peak, the cairn-topped Crohaun Mountain, and the Maum Pass immediately to its north. There may be an equinox sunrise alignment through the pass from this cairn.

The kist on its perimeter and the radially set kerbstones are rare, if not unique, features and it is only this monument's remoteness that has kept it from becoming

Glennafallia cairn, looking south with Dungarvan Bay to the left.

more widely known. For those that do not mind very steep climbs this is a must-see monument.

Mini-Gazetteer – 6.5km ESE there is a standing stone at **Dyrick**. 7.4km E there is a stone pair at Aughavanlomaun (County Cork). 12.7km E there is a stone row at **Knockboy**. 13.5km WSW there is a standing stone at **Knockcorragh**.

Glenwilliam
Standing Stone
OS Sheet 82: X 210 827

Directions: *Head north from Ardmore on the R673. Turn right at Lisakeelty crossroads approximately 6 kilometres from Ardmore (this is the sixth right turn.) After 600 metres you will reach a junction with a road from the right. The stone is in the field beyond this road, just 10 metres from the junction.*

Usually, when there is a standing stone at a junction, it is situated right alongside the road, but this one stands 10 metres into a neighbouring field. This raises the question of whether it has been moved to this location to provide a scratching post. This possibility is further hinted at by the way that the stone leans to the west.

The field hedges are quite tall and easily hide the stone from passing drivers, as it is only 1.5 metres tall. Only a 10-metre-long gap in the hedge to the west of the stone allows it to be seen easily.

Mini-Gazetteer – 1.7km NNW there is a fallen standing stone at **Boherboy**. 3.1km NE there is a standing stone at **Ahaun**. 7.9km E there is a court tomb at **Ballynamona Lower**.

Graigavalla
Standing Stone
OS Sheet 74: S 325 149

Directions: *From Carrick-on-Suir take the R680 south until you reach the R678. Turn onto the R678 and head west towards Clonmel. Two and a half kilometres along this road take the second road on the left. After 1 kilometre you will come to a sharp left-hand bend with a cul-de-sac straight ahead. Drive up the cul-de-sac and 2.5 kilometres along this road there is a track with two entrances (one through a brick gate and one next to the gate). Drive up this lane to the farmhouse. The standing stone is in a field 100 metres beyond the farmyard and is known as a fallen 'scratching post'.*

Glenwilliam standing stone. The stick is one metre long.

This stone lies in a field next to the track that descends from the pass known as The Gap and then leads across the Comeragh Mountains from the standing stone in **Carrigeen** TD. This now rather sad stone would not have stood much taller than 1.5 metres. It is rectangular in section and plan – 1 metre wide and 70 centimetres thick. Modern hedges block the views to the north, east and south, but nothing can really hide the Comeragh Mountains, which start to rise steeply just 500 metres to the south-west.

Mini–Gazetteer – 2.3km N there is a bullaun stone at **Killbrack**. 5.5km W there is a stone pair at **Knockanaffrin**. 8.7km WSW there is a barrow at **Tooreen West**. 10.5km ENE there is an 'oghamised' standing stone at **Crehanagh South**.

Gurteen Lower
Portal Tomb
OS Sheet 75: S 263 230

Directions: *From Carrick-on-Suir take the R680 west towards Clonmel and then the R706 towards Kilsheelan. Turn into the large gates on the left-hand side of the road after 400 metres. Continue along this track until you reach another track on the left leading to a farmhouse. Ask for permission and directions to the tomb at the farmhouse – not the large country house. As you will see from the description, it may not be worth the effort!*

Graigavalla standing stone, covered in silage, at the base of the picture. Beyond are the Comeragh Mountains.

This is one of the more ruinous portal tombs found in County Waterford. The capstone has become displaced and one of the portal stones has fallen. Today, the monument is very difficult to locate. It once stood below towering trees, but as these have fallen over the last fifteen to twenty years the sun has reached the ground and brambles have taken over. These now completely hide the tomb.

In 1897 Borlase quoted a good description of a much better monument:

> This monument consists of five standing stones, irregularly placed, supporting a large flag in an inclined position … The flag lies E. and W., and measures 9 feet 8 ins. From E. to W., and 8 feet 7 ins. from N. to S. … The area enclosed is 7 feet long by 4 feet broad.[50]

Clearly, the tomb was in much better condition then, with its capstone still in place. Of the capstone, Borlase quotes Ryland, saying 'that it wants the flatness and peculiar position of the more perfect of these works'.[51] (There's no pleasing some people.)

Just yards in front of the tomb is a small stream that feeds into the River Suir, which is just 400 metres to the north.

Mini-Gazetteer – 2.5km S there is a standing stone at *Cloghadda*. 8.8km S there is a stone pair at *Knockanaffrin*. 10km ESE there is a stone pair at *Ballinadysert*. 13km NNW there are two Sheela-na-Gigs at Fethard (County Tipperary).

Gurteen Lower
Standing Stone
OS Sheet 75: S 284 228

Directions: *From Carrick-on-Suir take the N24 west towards Clonmel. In Kilsheelan village turn south on the R706 and then west along the R680. The stone can be seen on the right-hand side of the road after a few hundred metres.*

The location of this stone is almost idyllic. In fact it is almost too idyllic. This is because it is at the edge of a country estate and the lands below it have been land-scaped. Below the stone, at the foot of the north-facing slope it stands on, is the flood plain of the River Suir, which flows past 500 metres to the north.

The stone is 1.5 metres tall and aligned east-west. It is very uneven in profile and may have been damaged in antiquity. From this stone it is easier to appreciate that the portal tomb to the west is actually situated on the Suir's flood plain.

Mini-Gazetteer – 2.1km W there is a portal tomb also in **Gurteen Lower** TD. 3km SW there is a standing stone at **Gurteen Upper**. 8.7km S there is a stone pair at **Knockanaffrin**. 9.5km ESE there is a portal tomb at **Sheskin**.

Gurteen Upper – Cloghadda
Standing Stone
OS Sheet 75: S 264 205

Directions: *From Clonmel follow the R680 eastwards. Two and a half kilometres outside the town there is a sharp right-hand bend. Take the next right, 500 metres past this bend. A little over 3 kilometres along this road you reach a right-hand turn with a track opposite that leads into a pine plantation. Park here and walk up the track for 300 metres looking out for the stone on the left-hand side of the track at the edge of the trees.*

Although it stands at the side of a forest track and is over 3 metres tall, this stone is easy to miss. This is because the trees near to it are crowding it out and smother-ing it with their lower branches. It is roughly square in cross section and reaches a gentle point.

The stone stands on a gentle south-west-facing slope at the far north end of the Comeragh Mountains. To the north-west, if the trees were not in the way, the views would take in the peak of Raven's Rock. To the south the stone overlooks a small valley formed by the River Glasha as it winds its way down to the River Suir.

Hopefully, when the trees in the surrounding plantation are cleared, the stone will one day be given a little bit of space, if not the restoration of its views.

Looking west past Gurteen Lower standing stone over the flood plains of the River Suir.

Gurteen Upper standing stone hiding in the trees.

Mini-Gazetteer – 2.5km N there is a portal tomb at ***Gurteen Lower***. 8km S there is a standing stone at ***Lyre***. 9.4km E there is a stone pair at ***Ballinadysert***. 15km E there is a portal tomb at ***Ballyquin***.

Harristown
Passage Tomb
OS Sheet 76: S 676 040

Directions: *Take the R683 east from Waterford and then the R684 south for 4.5 kilo-metres until you come to a left turn – take this road. After about 1 kilometre you will see a small track/drive on the left. Park here and walk along the track until you reach a gate leading into where the radio aerials are located. Pass through this enclosure and over the gate. Walk across the ridge to the far end where the tomb is located. There is a phone number on the far gate. Ring this number, prefixing it with (051), to ask if it is ok to enter.*

For me this is one of County Waterford's star sites. It may be ruinous, but its location is simply stunning! This important monument is located on the south end of a ridge that runs north-south with fantastic coastal views to the south and over the mouth of Waterford Harbour to the east. This tomb has been dated to the Bronze Age and, more than any other in the county, says a lot about the importance of sea travel to the occupants of the area in that period. Unlike most other passage tombs in Ireland the three in County Waterford (Harristown, **Matthewstown** and **Carriglong**) do not date from the Neolithic. In style these tombs have more in common with the monuments of Cornwall and the Scilly Isles than other Irish monuments. The link between Irish copper and Cornish tin could be massively important here (see main text).

J. Hawkes excavated the site in 1939. Although there were few finds the struc-ture of the monument proved very interesting. When the site was cleared a clay floor was discovered beneath it, which was considered natural, but 'likely that it had been prepared for the reception of the tomb'.[52] Fragments of charcoal were discovered upon this surface implying that the turf had been stripped from the area. A 7.5-centimetre layer of clay and charcoal was found in areas above this.

Before excavation twenty stones from the 10-metre-diameter kerb were visible. Further kerbstones and some empty sockets were revealed, making the original total twenty-nine stones in all. The stones creating the kerb were set in sockets 15-30 centimetres deep.

Outside of the kerb a previously unseen spread of cairn material was found. It was not possible to say if this was an original feature or whether it was added at a later date to accommodate the secondary burials found within it.

The passage and chamber are 7 metres in length. At the entrance, there is a gap of 1 metre between the walls, which is spanned by a sill stone. The rear of the chamber is 1.3 metres wide and blocked by a large septal slab. Echoing the divergence in width, the orthostats also rise in height from front to rear, climb-ing from 1 metre to 1.2 metres tall. The orthostats were found to be set into trenches cut into the clay floor from 45-60 centimetres deep. The inner faces of these trenches were vertical, while the outer faces sloped. This allowed stones to be packed behind the orthostats to hold them securely in place. This attention to

Above: Looking south-
west of the remains of
Harristown passage tomb.

Right: Plan of
Harristown, after J
Hawkes.

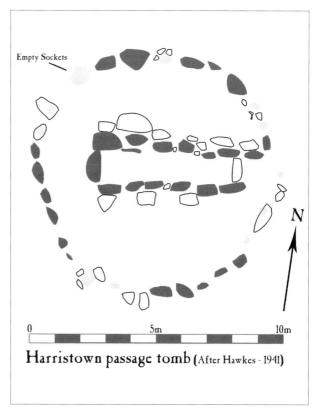

Empty Sockets

N

0   5m   10m

Harristown passage tomb (After Hawkes - 1941)

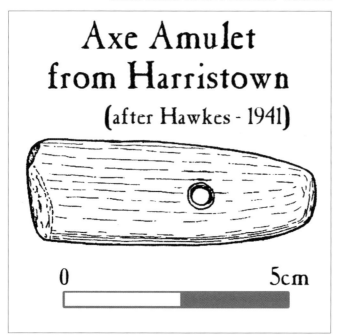

Axe-amulet from Harristown passage tomb.

detail in the construction techniques employed has surely helped in preserving the monument's condition.

Two primary cremations were found within the passage and chamber. Accompanying these were a stone-axe amulet and a similarly shaped pebble. Outside of this area several secondary burials were uncovered. These were placed both within and without the kerb. One of these was found with a food vessel and three of them were associated with cinerary urns. Also uncovered were a pigmy cup, a bronze blade, a stone bead and some bone pins. Outside the kerb, 1 metre from the entrance to the passage, a cremation pit was uncovered that contained the remains of three individuals.

Mini-Gazetteer – 5.6km SSW there is a standing stone at *Ballymacaw*. 8.6km W there is a passage tomb at *Carriglong*. 10.1km WNW there is a wedge tomb at *Munmahoge*. 14.3km W there is a standing stone at *Ballymote*.

Kealfoun
Standing Stone
OS Sheet 75: S 372 077

Directions: *From Kilmacthomas follow the R677 north for 300 metres and turn left and then left again. Continue for 2 kilometres and turn left at the crossroads after a church.*

Kealfoun standing stone, showing later
Christianisation.

Three hundred metres along on the left there is a school. The standing stone is in the field
behind the school, next to the playground's rear wall. Obviously, with this stone being so
close to a school, it is best to visit this site outside of school hours.

Being situated so close to a church it is no surprise to find several simple crosses
inscribed on this 1.5-metre-tall standing stone. It is located in a field, hidden
behind the rear wall of a school playground, and can only just be seen from the
road: its top barely showing above the wall.

Mini-Gazetteer – 2km WNW there is a stone pair at **Ashtown**. 4.1km SSW
there is a stone pair at **Garranmillon Lower** with ogham inscriptions. 10.4km
WNW there is a standing stone at **Carrigeen**. 11.4km WSW there are two cairns
at **Treenearla Commons**.

Kilbrack
Bullaun Stone
OS Sheet 75: S 326 172

Directions: *It is very difficult to give simple directions to this site. An Ordnance Survey*
map is recommended to find the track that leads to the site. One hundred metres after leav-
ing the main road there is a dirt track on the right. Follow this past the second gate. One

hundred metres after the second gate there is a double field gate on the right. Enter this field and follow the field hedge to the left. Where the bank turns left you should be able to see the bullaun stone on the opposite bank, next to a wooden post.

Here at Kilbrack there once stood an ecclesiastical site. All that remains now is half of the circular bank that surrounded the site and three bullaun stones. These are set into the bank. The largest, and only visible one, is a pear-shaped boulder that stands at a sharp turn in the bank. The 1.8 metre by 1.5 metre stone has two basins, which are at the thinner end of the stone. The more central bullaun is 25 centimetres in diameter and 15 centimetres deep. The other is smaller and shallower.

It is always difficult to say whether an ecclesiastical site was built at the location of bullaun stones, or if the bullauns were made for the church. However, certain locations do offer clues: here Crohaun Hill can just be seen standing proud on the northern horizon. Moving away from the site causes the hill to disappear.

Mini-Gazetteer – 4.3km NE there is a stone pair at ***Ballinadysert***. 8.6km E there is a standing stone and portal tomb at ***Ballyquin***. 9.7km SW there is a stone row at ***Tooreen West***. 14km NE there is a bullaun stone at Kilkieran (County Kilkenny).

Kilbrien Lower
Stone Pair
OS Sheet 75 & 82: S 246 044

Directions: *Although this site is not marked on the Ordnance Survey map, one is required to navigate the many small roads around this area. The stones are located just to the north-east of the 217-metre-point marked in the townland.*

Originally, this site may have been more than just a stone pair, as there is another small stone set in-line with them some 30 metres away. The taller of the two stones is 1 metre tall and 50 centimetres wide, with a rounded top. The other stone is only slightly shorter but has an asymmetrically pointed top.

The alignment of the pair's axis is towards the south-east and points in the direction of the base of the southern slopes of Crohaun Mountain. It is unlikely that there is a sunrise alignment at this point, but it is possible that the winter solstice sun may rise through the Maum Pass when viewed from here.

The ground rises gently to the west and actually blocks any view in that direction, but the whole of the ***Coumeraglin*** complex of monuments is visible to the east. It is possible to make out the ***Cutteen South/Coumaraglinmountain*** standing stone from here, some 3 kilometres to the east of, and 300 metres higher than, this site.

Mini-Gazetteer – 2.8km WNW there is a stone row at **Knockboy**. 5.5km NNW there is a stone row at **Reanadampaun Commons**. 9.4km W there is a standing stone at **Mweeling**. 12.9km SE there is a standing stone at **Sheskin**.

Kilbrack bullaun stone.

Kilbrien Lower stone pair with the Monavullagh Mountains in the distance.

Kilclooney standing stone.

Kilclooney
Standing Stone
OS Sheet 75: S 360 106

Directions: *From Carrick-on-Suir take the R676 south towards Lemybrien. Take the first right, 3.5 kilometres after crossing the R678. Continue to a T-junction and turn right. After 1 kilometre the road forks. Take the right-hand road. Three hundred metres along this road there is a farmyard on the left. Park near to this and walk back up the road and you will see the stone in the field to the right.*

With Croughaun Hill to the east and the Comeragh Mountains to the west this sub-2-metre-tall stone is in a great location. It is rectangular in section with its longest sides 90 centimetres long. These long sides are oriented north-east to south-west. The north side aligns to the northern slopes of Croughaun Hill and may present a summer solstice alignment.

There are several areas of the field around the stone that are not cut. This is because they contain many large stones. These are probably field clearance, but several of them do appear to be standing up. Was there a small complex of monuments here once?

Mini-Gazetteer – 1.1km SSE there is a stone pair at ***Ashtown***. 6.8km NNE is ***Mothel***, where County Waterford's only-known piece of rock art was found. 9.3km WSW there is a cairn at ***Cutteen North***. 10.2km NE there is an ogham stone at ***Ballyquin***.

Looking into Kilgreany Cave.

Kilgreany
Cave
OS Sheet 82: X 176 944

Directions: *From Dungarvan take the R672 and then the N72 west towards Lismore. Turn south down the R671 and take the second left-hand turn. Continue for 3 kilometres and turn left again. Go as far as the T-junction and turn left. After 300 metres there is a farm track on the right. This can be identified by the road in front of it having been widened with hardcore verges. Drive up this track to the farm and ask for directions.*

Kilgreany Cave is ranked amongst the most important caves in Ireland. It has undergone two excavations: firstly in 1928 by E.K. Tratman with the Bristol Speleological Society and again in 1934 by H.L. Movius and a team from the Harvard Archaeological Expedition. These excavations uncovered evidence that the cave had been in use for over 6,500 years. Apart from animal bones, such as Irish elk, lynx, arctic lemming and bear, that had been washed down into the cave, several burials were discovered. The two most significant of these were two full inhumations. One of these was found next to a hearth that contained the bones of animals that would have inhabited the area in the Ice Age. This led the excavators to believe they had found what they had been looking for – evidence of humanity in Ireland from the Palaeolithic era. In the 1980s radiocarbon-dating tests were undertaken on the bones, which concluded that they were from the Neolithic.[53] Ireland's oldest person had not been found at Kilgreany Cave.

In the Bronze Age the cave was once again used for burials and, in the Late Bronze Age, it was used for the deposition of votive offerings. A total of twenty-two individuals may be represented by the remains discovered.

Another uncovered skeleton, a male known as Kilgreany B, showed signs of trauma to the skull. There were further signs of trauma found on other deposits: a fragment of skull from a juvenile had two unhealed wounds caused by a sharp edge. The female skeleton, known as Kilgreany A, had signs of an injury from a sharp weapon to her jaw.[54]

Other items found create a timeline of occupation and ritual use of this cave spanning 6,500 years. There are few places in Ireland that have that pedigree.

The cave is in a limestone escarpment. To enter it you must scramble down a steep, loose slope. The entrance is 6 metres high, 5 metres wide at the base and shaped like an inverted V. The main space is 6 metres deep with smaller channels running back into the hillside, one of which does emerge to the rear of the main entrance.

Mini-Gazetteer – 10.5km SSE there is a standing stone at **Boherboy.** 11.6km NNE there is a stone row at **Knockboy**. 12.2km SSE there is a standing stone at **Glenwilliam**. 15.5km NNW there is a cairn at **Glennafallia**.

Killbarrymeaden
Standing Stone
OS Sheets 75 & 82: S 460 031

Directions: *From the village of Kill head east along the R681 for 500 metres. On the right-hand side of the road you will see a fenced-in plant, possibly a small water treatment facility. The stone is in the field opposite this enclosure and can be seen from the road.*

This is a small stone with hedge-restricted views. It is 1 metre tall and no more than 1 metre wide. The reeds growing around it are almost as tall as the stone.

Although the nearby hedgerows limit the views from the stone itself, from the road it is possible to see a high rocky outcrop to the north of the site. Obviously, there is no solar alignment with this outcrop, but its dominant position may have had some relevance in choosing its location.

Mini-Gazetteer – 1.5km ESE there is a portal tomb at **Savagetown**. 4.9km E there is a stone pair at **Croagh**. 9.7km NW there is a stone row at **Rathmaiden**. 12km ENE there is a portal tomb at **Knockeen**.

Outcrop of rock visible from Killbarrymeaden standing stone.

Knockanaffrin
Stone Circle
OS Sheet 75: S 266 142

Directions: *You will a GPS to locate this circle. When you are approaching its position look for a small area at the base of a rocky, gorse-covered slope, surrounded by a low wall. The stones of this new stone circle can be seen rising slightly above the grass.*

I stumbled across this previously unrecorded site while approaching the stone pair in the same townland. The low stones are difficult to make out, as they only just stand proud of the grass. Once located, a clear pattern of small stones arranged in a circle can be seen, with a broader stone at the south-west. This makes it an axial stone circle. It is approximately 10 metres in diameter.

The site is on a small plateau at the base of a rocky bank. The small, odd-shaped field that the stones are in seems to indicate that the walls were erected with the knowledge that the stone circle existed. There are extensive views to the west towards the Knockmealdown Mountains.

Mini-Gazetteer – 6.7km ENE there is a bullaun stone at **Kilbrack**. 10.2km SSW there is a stone row at **Knockboy**. 10.7km ESE there is a standing stone at **Ashtown**. 12.6km S there is a standing stone at **Crohaun**.

Knockanaffrin stone circle, looking south-west.

Knockanaffrin
Stone Pair
OS Sheet 75: S 270 142

Directions: *You will need an Ordnance Survey map to locate this site. It is best approached from the road to the west. Where the road meets a farm track there is a bungalow on the right. Ask here for access. Follow the track beyond this house to a small cottage. From the gate above this cottage you should be able to see some ruins diagonally to the right. Walk past the cottage and continue until you see the stones.*

Reaching this monument is a bit of a pilgrimage: a 1-kilometre walk up steep slopes past ruined farmhouses and ancient field systems. The journey is also a history lesson in itself. Starting at the base of the hill there is the modern farmhouse. Halfway up you pass a smaller cottage and then, just below the stones, there is a ruined farmhouse and barn complex. Taken in reverse, these three house sites demonstrate a standard pattern that can be observed throughout Ireland. Initially, with no mechanical transport, it was important for farmers to live in the centre of their land, hence the earliest house being halfway up the mountain. Then it was possible to move closer to the road, but not much further down the mountain. Now, with quad bikes and tractors it is possible for farmers to live at the edge of their land and closer to the road.

Even without the above, the climb to these stones is well rewarded. Not only are the views tremendous, but the two main stones are also excellent. Whether the two 1.5-metre-tall stones constitute a stone pair is an interesting point, because nearby, a small 40-centimetre-tall stone seems to be in-line with them – is it a stone row?

Knockanaffrin stone pair, looking west.

The main stones stand 1.5 metres apart and are aligned north-east to south-west on a small promontory on the western slopes of the Monavullagh Mountains. Looking westward the Knockmealdown Mountains can be seen.

Mini-Gazetteer – 1.7km S there is a standing stone at **Lyre**. 1.9km SE there is a standing stone at **Carrigeen**. 8.8km N there is a portal tomb at **Gurteen Lower**. 14.5km SW there is a standing stone at **Mweeling**.

Knockboy
Stone Row
OS Sheets 75 & 82: S 219 05

Directions: *From Dungarvan take the R672 north. Turn right onto the N25 and then rejoin the R672 heading north. Five and a half kilometres along this road there is a sweeping right-hand bend followed by a left-hand bend after a further 500 metres. The road then straightens out. Continue along and turn right at the first crossroads. After 800 metres you pass through Knockboy village. The stones are on the left-hand side of the road 250 metres past a farm track to the right.*

The three stones comprising this row stand in a small field. A fourth stone lies next to them. The row is aligned north-east to south-west with the tallest stone at the south-west. This configuration is similar to many of the stone rows found in County Cork.

The smallest upright stone is 60 centimetres tall and the tallest is 1.5 metres in height. The recumbent stone looks as if it may have once been part of the row, as there

Knockboy stone row.

is a gap in this position, but it was apparently moved to this location from nearby.[55] The whole row is just 5 metres long with very little space between the adjacent stones.

There is the possibility of an interesting alignment from this row. To the east there is a standing stone in the saddle between Seefin and Farbreaga, two peaks in the Monavullagh Mountains. There are also three cairns on Seefin just to the north of this saddle and any of these monuments could be markers of significant sunrises when viewed from Knockboy.

When visiting here it is also worth making a trip to Knockboy church to the south-east. This has several ogham stones incorporated into its structure.

Mini-Gazetteer – 6.6km ESE there is a standing stone at **Crohaun**. 9.7km NE there is a standing stone at **Carrigeen**. 10.3km NNE there is a stone pair at **Knockanaffrin**. 15km ENE there is a stone pair at **Ashtown**.

Knockcorragh
Standing Stone
OS Sheet 74: R 965 036

Directions: *You will need an Ordnance Survey map and a compass or GPS to locate this site. It is best to approach from the lane to the east.*

This is the eastern-most of two standing stones marked on the Ordnance Survey map. The other is either built into a low field wall or has been removed: the stone

Knockcorragh standing stone with the wall of rock behind it.

in a wall close to the location marked on the Ordnance Survey map may not be the other standing stone.

This stone is a small, leaning slab that is 1 metre tall, 1.2 metres wide and aligned east-west. As a standing stone it is remarkably unspectacular, however, its hilltop location is quite amazing. Five metres south of the stone a 2-metre-tall ridge of exposed rock runs across the hill from east to west. The southern side of this ridge is rough and broken up, but the north side has a smooth concave surface. This gives it the appearance of being a petrified tidal wave. Naturally occurring erosion processes have broken up a section of this rocky ridge, 30 metres south of the standing stone, into large slabs. This looks like it could have been a handy source of megalithic building material. A study of this rock and that used in monuments in the area could produce interesting results. Such a formation would surely have seemed special or even sacred by our Neolithic ancestors.

Knockeen
Portal Tomb
OS Sheets 75 & 76: S 575 065

Directions: *Head south on the N25 from Waterford and take the first left after passing the R686 junction. Take the second left and continue for about 1 kilometre until you see a farm on your left. Opposite this is a gate into a field and the tomb is visible from here.*

Knockeen portal tomb.

Revd R.H. Ryland summed up this monument perfectly:

> At Sugar-loaf Hill, so-called from its abrupt and conical shape, there is a noble
> Cromlech, or Druid's altar, the most perfect of these antiquities, which is to be
> found in the county.[56]

Ryland was obviously suitably impressed and went on to astutely note:

> Connected with this relic, we have here an undisputable instance of the policy
> of those who first introduced Christianity into this country; and who, in every
> case, endeavoured to engraft the pure religion upon the heathen superstition which
> preceded it. The neighbourhood of a Celtic monument was selected as the site of a
> Christian church, which now in its turn affords protection to its neglected rival.

Knockeen is not only one of the finest portal tombs in Waterford, but must be
ranked amongst the best in Ireland. Its form is extremely impressive, with double
capstones held 5 metres above the ground. The smaller capstone rests on the walls of
the chamber and in turn supports one end of the larger capstone. The west end of
the upper capstone rests on the portal stones, which frame a full-height doorstone.

The monument is built into a field boundary, which also happens to be the
wall around the church mentioned above. Access to the chamber is via a small
kennel-hole-like gap between the stone that forms the south wall of the chamber
and the backstone.

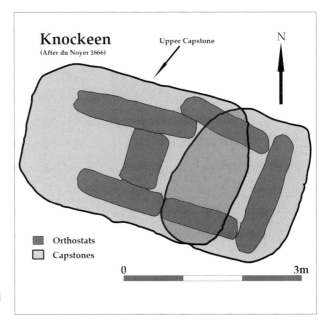

Plan of Knockeen portal
tomb, after Du Noyer.

Choosing this location for the site of the church must have been influenced by
the importance of the portal tomb at the time of the church's construction. Sadly,
no folklore exists to give hints as to why the tomb was so important.

Mini-Gazetteer – 4km WNW there is a standing stone at **Whitfield North**.
5.8km SW there is a passage tomb at **Matthewstown**. 10.4km ESE there is a
passage tomb at **Harristown**. 15.9km N there is a wedge tomb at Ballyvatheen
(County Kilkenny).

Lagnagoushee
Standing Stone
OS Sheet 82: X 257 846

Directions: *This site requires an Ordnance Survey map to find.*

This standing stone is very similar to the one at **Boherboy**. It has even fallen over to
look more like it. It now lies on a wide plateau with extensive views in all directions. A nearby barn ruins any ambience that the stone may once have offered.

Mini-Gazetteer – 3km WNW there is a standing stone at **Ahaun**. 5.5km W
there is a standing stone at **Boherboy**. 12.7km NW there is a cave at **Kilgreany**.
14.7km NE there is a standing stone at **Sheskin**.

The fallen Lagnagoushee standing stone.

Lyre standing stone seen from across the valley.

Lyre
Standing Stone
OS Sheet 75: S 268 125

Directions: *This site requires a GPS and Ordnance Survey map to find.*

This stone is not marked on the Ordnance Survey map and is difficult to access. It is approximately 1.5 metres tall and stands on an east-facing slope overlooking

Matthewstown passage tomb.

a steep-sided river valley. It could be the remains of a stone row/pair, as there is a recumbent stone of similar size 10 metres away from it.

Mini-Gazetteer – 2.1km WSW there is a stone circle at *Tooreen*. 8km N there is a standing stone at *Cloghadda*. 9.8km ESE there is a standing stone at *Ashtown*. 10.5km N there is a portal tomb at *Gurteen Lower*.

Matthewstown
Passage Tomb
OS Sheets 75 & 76: S 529 029

Directions: *From Tramore take the R682 north. At the third crossroads turn left, continue for nearly 3 kilometres until you come to a tarmac track on the left. Opposite is one of Waterford's little dolmen signs. Head up this track until you come to a weighbridge. The tomb is behind this.*

Alongside *Harristown* and *Carriglong*, this monument is one of the undifferentiated passage tombs in County Waterford. It is less complete than the others in some ways, but it does retain most of its roof-stones. Being on Waterford's signposted 'Dolmen Trail' it is the most accessible of the trio.

The chamber and remains of the truncated passage are 3.5 metres long and covered by three roof-stones. To the west of the chamber's backstone, there is an arc of four kerbstones. The curvature of these would suggest a cairn diameter of approximately

Monaneea standing stone. The stick is one metre long.

10 metres. Five orthostats make up each side of the remains, but there would have been more originally if the passage reached the eastern edge of the projected kerb.

The ridge that the monument stands on offers fine views if you can ignore the heavily industrialised factory to the immediate east. Beyond these buildings are the Ballyscanlan Hills, on the opposite side of which lies the **Carrickavrantry** wedge tomb. To the west the Monavullagh and Comeragh Mountains make up the horizon.

Mini-Gazetteer – 1.9km NNE there is a large standing stone in **Ballymoat** TD. 3.4km W there is a portal tomb at **Ballynageeragh**. 6.9km W there is a standing stone at **Killbarrymeaden**. 14.1km ENE there is a double cist at **Ballygunnertemple**.

Monaneea
Standing Stone
OS Sheet 82: X 225 848

Directions: *Head north from Ardmore on the R673. Turn right at Lisakeelty crossroads approximately 6 kilometres from Ardmore (this is the sixth right turn.) Turn left at the next crossroads and continue 300 metres past a sharp right-hand bend. This stone is 300 metres into the field on the left-hand side of the road and is clearly visible.*

Mothel rock art, now kept at Cork University.

If you were asked to quickly draw a standing stone, you would probably draw something that looks like this one. It is a very generic-looking example: 1.5 metres tall, smooth sided with a rounded top and near-rectangular cross section. Its size and uniformity are in total contrast to the huge, bulky stone in **Ahaun** TD, 500 metres to the north.

The fields around it are subdivided by a criss-cross of electric fences and the ground is very boggy. This makes reaching the stone a very muddy exercise.

Mini-Gazetteer – 500m N there is a standing stone at **Ahaun**. 2.4km WSW there is a standing stone at **Boherboy**. 6.4km E there is a court tomb at **Ballynamona Lower**. 16.6km SSW there is a cairn at **Crohaun**.

Mothel
Rock Art
OS Sheet: Not applicable – now housed in the Stone Corridor at Cork University

This is the only piece of rock art to have been found in County Waterford and sadly it no longer resides in the county. It was 'donated' to Cork University by Revd Power in the early 1900s. It was originally to go to the National Museum in Kildare Street, Dublin, but for some reason it was diverted to Cork.

It was first noticed by a passer-by who saw it incorporated into a wall. It remained there for some years until it was brought to the attention of Revd Power, who presented a paper about the stone in 1907.

The stone is 1 metre by 1 metre in size with carvings on a curved surface. The decoration consists of ten or more cup and ring motifs that abut each other and cover most of one surface. The majority of the design is made up of a cup and one ring: there is just one double-ringed cup. There appears to be some damage to the carved surface, which means some motifs may have been lost.

Munmahoge
Wedge Tomb
OS Sheets 75 & 76: S 577 061

Directions: *Head south on the N25 from Waterford and take the first left after passing the R686 junction. Take the second left and then take the right-hand road where it forks. At the next crossroads turn right. Four hundred metres along this road you will come to a farmyard on the right. Ask here for access to 'Munmahoge Dolmen'.*

It is not surprising that this monument is one of the least visited in County Waterford. It stands on the opposite side of a small valley to the amazing portal tomb at **Knockeen** and is completely hidden inside a wide field boundary. Luckily, there is a small clearing within the hedge that allow for easy access. However, its position does make it difficult to find.

The tomb is located at the top of a north-facing slope overlooking a small stream that separates it from the nearby portal tomb. The portal tomb is easily visible from the site and to the north-west you would be able to see the bulbous rocky outcrop known locally as the Sugar Loaf if it wasn't for the intervening hedgerows and trees.

The remains of the 3-metre-long gallery are aligned east-west, with the east end embedded in the bank that forms part of the boundary. One roof-stone remains in place and two large stones, now built into the bank, may be displaced roof-stones. The orthostats forming the southern side of the gallery are all present, but the other side has had several stones removed. There are no end stones visible and there are no traces of a cairn or mound around the monument.

Mini-Gazetteer – 450m NNW there is a portal tomb at **Knockeen**. 5.8km WSW there is a passage tomb at **Matthewstown**. 10.9km WSW there is a portal tomb at **Savagetown**. 12.7km WSW there is a standing stone at **Ballingary**.

The single capstone over the gallery of Munmahoge wedge tomb.

Mweeling
Standing Stone
OS Sheets 74 & 82: S 153 057

Directions: *From Dungarvan follow the signs for Lismore along the R672 and then the N72. Six and a half kilometres along the N72 turn right onto the R671 in the direction of Clonmel. Five kilometres on you will go around a hairpin bend. Turn left at the next opportunity. Following this road will bring you to Dyrick Hill. Continue for 1 kilometre past the hill until you see a gate on the right-hand side of the road. The stone can be seen from this gate.*

The view to the south of this 1.2-metre-tall stone looks towards Dyrick Hill, which has several standing stones around it (see *Dyrick* above). This craggy, scruffy stone culminates in a rough, jagged point. At the base of the stone there are several exposed packing stones.

Between the stone and Dyrick Hill, the land drops from the boggy plateau that it stands on to a small valley, which rises up to the base of the hill. To the north and west, rocky slopes obscure the views, but the vista remains open to the east towards the Monavullagh Mountains.

Mini-Gazetteer – 1km S there is a standing stone at *Dyrick*. 6.6km E there is a stone row at *Knockboy*. 9.4km E there is a stone pair at *Kilbrien Lower*. 11.2km ENE there is a stone row at *Tooreen West*.

Mweeling standing stone.

Park
Bullaun Stone
OS Sheet 75: S 308 185

Directions: *From Clonmel take the R680 east towards Carrick-on-Suir. Take the second right-hand turn after passing the R706. Continue along this road, making sure to bear left at a Y-junction. Turn left towards Rathgormack. Three hundred metres along the R706 there is a gate on the left. The bullaun is in this field, but parking near here is difficult.*

This is a thick sub-rectangular slab with two bullauns/basins set symmetrically in its upper surface. Each of the bullauns is 25 centimetres in diameter and 10 centimetres deep. The slab now stands on one edge, fortunately with the bullauns showing, against a pile of field clearance. The rocks that make up this heap could be the remains of early monastic buildings that stood nearby.

The bullaun stone once stood next to the small, babbling brook that runs across the south edge of the field.

Mini-Gazetteer – 4.8km WNW there is a standing stone at **Gurteen Upper**. 10.4km E there is a portal tomb at **Ballyquin**. 12.6km ESE there is a portal tomb at **Whitestown East**. 14.9km ENE there is a portal tomb at Ballyhenebery (County Kilkenny).

Park bullaun stone.

Powersknock
Standing Stone
OS Sheets 75 & 76: S 522 084

Directions: *From Waterford take the N25 west and then the R681 south. After about 400 metres you will come to a left-hand bend in the road. The stone is just before this on the left-hand side of the road 50 metres into the field.*

If this slab-like standing stone was on more open ground it would be rather impressive, but situated where it is (in a roadside field, surrounded by high trees), any potential presence is lost.

The field does not seem to be in use and nettles and weeds surround the stone's base, obscuring much of it from view. The stone is 1.7 metres tall and set well back from the road, near to a dangerous bend on the R681.

Mini-Gazetteer – 2.8km SE there is a portal tomb at **Gaulstown**. 6km ESE there is a wedge tomb at **Munmahoge**. 11.1km WNW there is a portal tomb at **Whitestown East**. 14.5km NW there is an ogham stone at **Ballyquin**.

Powersknock standing stone.

Raheens
Stone Pair
OS Sheet 75: S 512 071

Directions: *Take the N25 west from Waterford and then turn south along the R681. Take the first right-hand turn and then bear left at the next fork in the road. After 500 metres the road veers to the right. Shortly after this bend there is a farm track on the left. The stones are 300 metres along this track in the field to the left.*

Only one of the two stones from this pair seems to still be standing. Looking at how slender the remaining stone is, it is possible that cattle broke the other one by using it as a scratching post.

The remaining stone is over 2 metres tall and not much more than 20 centimetres thick.

Mini-Gazetteer – 1.6km NE there is a standing stone at ***Powersknock***. 2.9km ESE there is a portal tomb at ***Gaulstown***. 6km SW there is a portal tomb at ***Savagetown***. 9.2km E there is a standing stone at ***Ballindud***.

Rathmaiden
Stone Row
OS Sheet 75: S 384 092

Directions: *From Kilmacthomas follow the R677 north for 300 metres and turn left and then left again. Continue on for 2 kilometres and turn right at the crossroads. After 1.5*

One of the Raheens stones.

Rathmaiden stone row, looking west.

kilometres there is a new bungalow on the right with a high wooden fence along its northern boundary. Immediately beyond this fence there is a field gate. Walk through this gate to the top of the field and into the next field. Turn right and go to the next field along. The stone row is on the left 30 metres from the entrance to this field.

Situated on a plateau/wide ridge to the east of Crohaun Mountain this site offers splendid views. While the mountain dominates to the west, there is an extensive vista to the east that is interrupted slightly by the gently rising fields. The Ordnance Survey map shows a standing stone by the roadside to the west of the row, but does not indicate the row's presence. There is no standing stone.

Four out of six stones remain standing, with the other two lying on the ground where they fell. They are aligned roughly north-west to south-east and do not quite align to the highest point of Crohaun, but to a position somewhere on its southern slopes.

The tallest upright stone is 1.8 metres tall and the shortest is a little over 1 metre high. They have almost been incorporated into a field boundary, which was actually erected a very short distance from the stones. The trees and bushes from this ditch are starting to hide the monument and two of the stones now have a coat of ivy.

Oddly, the second stone from the south-east end of the row is not in-line with the other stones – a peculiar feature that may even be unique amongst rows of this length.

Mini-Gazetteer – 2.4km W there is a standing stone at *Ashtown*. 9.3km NNE there is a portal tomb at *Ballyquin*. 11.1km NNE there is an ogham stone at *Crehanagh South*. 12.5km WSW there are a number of cairns at *Coumaraglinmountain*.

Reanadampaun Commons – The Tampauns
Stone Row
OS Sheet 75: S 220 094

Directions: *From Dungarvan take the R672 north. Turn right onto the N25 and then rejoin the R672 heading north. Five and a half kilometres along this road there is a sweeping right-hand bend followed by a left-hand bend after a further 500 metres. The road then straightens out. Continue on and turn right at the second crossroads. Take the first left and then the second right and go as far as the T-junction. Turn left. One kilometre along this road there is a driveway on the left with white-brick gates. Ask at the farmhouse for access.*

This six-stone stone row is now incorporated into one side of a field boundary. A lone stone on the opposite side does not look as if it came from the row and is probably field clearance.

Reanadampaun stone row.

The arrangement of the north-east- to south-west-aligned row does not have a rational pattern, which is unusual. They do comprise three similar-sized and similar-shaped stones though. Perhaps it was not originally a stone row, but a stone circle that was disassembled and built into the ditch. Or, perhaps it was a stone row and moved into the field boundary. The direction of the alignment is a common one amongst stone rows, however, which does speak for it being original.

From the southern end the stones are: two large uneven conglomerates, a large squared-off block, a small slender stone, another squared-off block, and finally another small slender stone. The latter is hidden behind a tree and is very easy to miss.

Mini-Gazetteer – 1.3km NW there are two barrows at **Castlereagh**. 5.8km ENE there is a standing stone at **Lyre**. 7km ENE there is a standing stone at **Carrigeen**. 10.3km SSE there is a cairn at **Crohaun**.

Savagetown
Portal Tomb
OS Sheets 75 & 82: S 474 025

Directions: *From Waterford take the N25 west and then the R681 south. Take the fifth left turn. The portal tomb is about 1.2 kilometres along on the right.*

Savagetown portal tomb.

It is very difficult to work out what remains of this monument. It is heavily embedded in a large field boundary, with only the massive 3-metre-long capstone, a portal stone and one chamber wall-stone showing. What can be seen indicates that this could have been comparable to **Gaulstown** portal tomb 7.5 kilometres away.

In a similar fashion to the portal tombs in **Knockeen** and **Gaulstown** TDs, there is a large rocky outcrop within view of the monument.

Mini-Gazetteer – 3.1km E there is a portal tomb at **Dunhill**. 8.9km NE there is a standing stone at **Whitfield North**. 11.2km NW there is a stone row at **Rathmaiden**. 14.2km ENE there is a portal tomb at **Ballindud**.

Scartnadrinnymountain 1
Cairn
OS Sheets 75 & 82: Grid Ref: S 256 052

Directions: *An Ordnance Survey map is required to locate this site.*

Situated in a shallow col between a rocky outcrop to the south and the towering cliff face of a much larger rock prominence to the north, this cairn is in a great location. Sadly it has become covered in knee-high heather, and bracken is now starting to encroach upon it. It is only discernable from a distance by a rise in the heather which

Looking over Scartnadrinnymountain (1) cairn towards Crohaun Mountain.

covers it. Once upon the mound it is possible to see the stones with which it has been constructed. The cairn is 8 metres in diameter and has a slight hollow at the centre.

The site has extensive views to the west and the archaeological complexes in *Coumaraglinmountain* TD are visible to the east. Above these the tor on the peak of Seefin Mountain and the standing stone in *Cutteen South* TD are also visible. However, the cairns on Seefin in *Cutteen North* and *Cutteen South* are too low to be seen.

Mini-Gazetteer – 1.4km ESE there is a stone circle at *Coumaraglinmountain*. 4km SSE there is a standing stone at *Crohaun*. 6.4km N there is a barrow at *Tooreen West*. 9.7km E there is an 'oghamised' stone pair at *Garranmillon Lower*.

Scartnadrinnymountain 2
Cairn
OS Sheets 75 & 82: S 256 052

Directions: *An Ordnance Survey map is required to locate this site.*

A modern forestry track has obliterated one side of this possible cairn. All that can be seen here is an arc of stones that may have formed part of a kerb. There is no trace of a structure within this arc, so it was possibly once a stone circle rather

Possible kerbstones of Scartnadrinnymountain (2) cairn.

than a cairn. There is, however, a drystone wall just 5 metres away, which may have been built from the cairn material. This seems unlikely though, because the cairn on the opposite side of the wall does not appear to have been extensively robbed.

Close to these stones there are several others that appear to form alignments. These only protrude 30 centimetres above the peat, so it is hard to know for certain if they are standing stones. The peat could be hiding much more: perhaps a significant and extensive complex of circles and rows similar to those found at Beaghmore, County Tyrone.

Sheskin
Portal Tomb
OS Sheet 75: S 376 200

Directions: *From Carrick-on-Suir take the R680 west for 3 kilometres. Turn left 100 metres past a sharp right-hand bend. One and a half kilometres along this road turn left and continue to bear to the left. After 400 metres there is a farm track on the left. Drive along this track until you see the remains of the tomb on the right-hand side of the lane.*

This small, ruined portal tomb stands at the side of a farm lane. The chamber has collapsed and the 2-metre-square capstone has slipped so that one end now rests on the ground. Small portal stones that are just over 1 metre tall support the other end. These portal stones appear to be taller, as the site is raised above the trackway that passes immediately alongside.

The portal stones and doorstone of Sheskin portal tomb.

Alongside **Ballindud** portal tomb, this is another example that perhaps demonstrates that **Ballyquin** portal tomb may once have been a more portal tomb-like structure.

Mini-Gazetteer – 1.7km W there is a stone pair at **Ballinadysert**. 8.2km ENE there is a portal tomb at Ballyhenebery (County Kilkenny). 11.1km W there is a standing stone at **Cloghadda**. 12.3km S there is a standing stone at **Kilfoun**.

Sheskin
Standing Stone
OS Sheet 82: X 346 963

Directions: *From Ballyvoyle take the road east towards Stradbally for 700 metres. The standing stone is in the field opposite the right-hand junction at this point.*

This short standing stone occupies a spot in the centre of a large field. It is a little over 1 metre tall and can become hidden by long grass during the summer.

The views to the north-west are very impressive, taking in the Monavullagh Mountains. To the north-east lie the open plains of east Waterford.

Mini-Gazetteer – 5.4km NNE are the **Drumlohan** ogham stones. 8.9km NW there is a standing stone at **Crohaun**. 9.1km NW there are three cairns at **Treenearla Commons**. 14km SSW there is a court tomb at **Ballynamona Lower**.

Sheskin standing stone, looking north.

Tooreen
Stone Circle
OS Sheet 75: S 249 11z

Directions: *An Ordnance Survey map will be required in order to locate the complex at Tooreen Woods. The final road to the woods is difficult to find, as it runs alongside a bungalow and does not look like a public track. Once on this track, follow it until you pass through a gate. The stone circle is on the left-hand side of the road 50 metres from the gate.*

Once in Tooreen Woods this site is easy to locate, as it is just to one side of the main track through the woods. It has its own very small clearing in the trees, which is open to the road allowing it to be seen.

The remains of this circle are 4 metres in diameter. Many of its stones are missing, but there are no major gaps along its circumference. The stones appear to rise in size equally on each side as they progress around the circle. The tallest stone is no more than 50 centimetres high.

The pine trees that surround the circle on three sides block all the views to the river valley to the east and Knockanaffrin Mountain beyond. Like all plantation-bound sites it is a lottery visiting here, but you may be lucky and find the site cleared of the trees around it and its views opened up.

Mini-Gazetteer – 3.4km ENE there is a standing stone at *Carrigeen*. 10km SSE there is a standing stone at *Treenearla Commons*. 11.3km SSE there is a cairn at *Crohaun*. 11.8km SW there is a standing stone at *Dyrick*.

Tooreen stone circle hiding in the bracken.

Tooreen West
Barrow
OS Sheet 75: S 245 115

Directions: *See previous page. From the stone row, follow the signs. These will lead you along the ditch and back down through the woods to the barrow.*

Despite being in the middle of a pine plantation this barrow is easy to find, as it is in a clearing and is part of a signposted walk around Tooreen Woods. The hardest part is finding the woods. The 6-metre-diameter mound is not much more than 40 centimetres high and is surrounded by a barely discernable shallow fosse or ditch. The monument can be made out as a low, heather-covered bump with a circle of grass around it that indicates the ditch. There is a short row of standing stones to one side of the barrow, which may be an original feature.

Mini-Gazetteer – 3.7km NE there is a stone pair at **Knockanaffrin**. 6.8km SSW there is a stone row at **Knockboy**. 10km SSE there are several cairns at **Treenearla Commons**. 11.3km SSE there is a cairn at **Crohaun**.

Tooreen West
Stone Row
OS Sheet 75: S 246 117

Directions: *See previous page. From the stone circle walk along the track. On the right-hand side you will see a wooden stump with an arrow pointing to a track through the*

Tooreen West stone row.

woods. Follow this track until you reach a fence. The style to cross this fence is a bit rickety, so be careful. Once over the fence, turn left and follow the ditch.

This attractive stone row stands on a shelf on the southern slopes of a small, round hill. The largest stone is 1.1 metres tall and the smallest is just 40 centimetres high. The two stones in between decrease in size accordingly. The site overlooks the other monuments within the Tooreen Woods complex, which include a barrow and a stone circle.

The stones are aligned north-west to south-east, with the largest stone at the north-west. The style of the row, with its regularly decreasing-sized stones, gives it affinities with many stone rows in County Cork.

Mini-Gazetteer – 2.3km ENE there is a standing stone at **Lyre**. 7.6km SSE there is a group of cairns at **Coumaraglinmountain**. 9km NNE there is a standing stone at **Cloghadda**. 11.4km N there is a portal tomb at **Gurteen Lower**.

Treenearla Commons 1
Cairn
OS Sheet 75 & 82: S 274 019

Directions: *Finding this cairn is very difficult and requires a bit of luck and good light. It is not really worth the effort.*

Looking west towards the Knockmealdown Mountains from Treenearla Commons (2) cairn.

There is not a great deal to see of this cairn. It is situated on a small plateau on a south-facing slope below the two much larger cairns in this townland. Its presence is only betrayed by the very low bump that is covered in the different vegetation of its surroundings.

Mini-Gazetteer – 300m Grid Ref: S there is a standing stone at **Crohaun**. 8.1km ENE there is a stone pair at **Garranmillon Lower**. 10.8km N there is a standing stone at **Carrigeen**. 12.7km WNW there is a standing stone at **Mweeling**.

Treenearla Commons 2
Cairn
OS Sheet 75 & 82: S 273 020

Directions: *From Lemybrien follow the N25 south for 1.5 kilometres and turn right at Downey's Crossroads. At the next T-junction turn left and then left again at the next. A little over 1 kilometre along this road, turn right onto the pass road. After 3.5 kilometres there is a parking area on the left. Continue past this for 800 metres until you reach a lane to the left that heads south towards some radio masts on the top of Crohaun Hill. Park here. The two large cairns here can be found on the top of the rise on the opposite side of the road to the track up the hill.*

In terms of condition this cairn is not exactly fantastic, but its location is stunning. The majority of Treenearla Commons TD occupies a large plateau at the south-

Crohaun Mountain seen over Treenearla Commons (3) cairn.

ern end of the Monavullagh Mountains, just to the north of Croagh Mountain, overlooking Maum Pass. There are extensive views to the east and west.

The monument consists of a 1-metre-high pile of moderately sized rocks and is 15 metres in diameter.

Treenearla Commons 3
Cairn
OS Sheets 75 & 82: S 273 019

Directions: *From Lemybrien follow the N25 south for 1.5 kilometres and turn right at Downey's Crossroads. At the next T-junction turn left and then left again at the next. A little over 1 kilometre along this road turn right onto the pass road. After 3.5 kilometres there is a parking area on the left. Continue past this for 800 metres until you reach a lane to the left that heads south towards some radio masts on the top of Crohaun Hill. Park here. The two large cairns can be found on the top of the rise on the opposite side of the road to the track up the hill.*

The creation of walkers' shelters from the large stones of this cairn makes it look larger than it actually is. At over 20 metres in diameter and 2 metres high, it is still large enough to make it worth visiting. It is located at the extreme south edge of a large plateau overlooking the Maum Pass. There are extensive views along the pass to the east and west and Croagh Mountain dominates the view to the south.

Treenearla Commons standing stone.

Treenearla Commons 4
Standing Stone
OS Sheets 75 & 82: S 271 018

The ground around this standing stone is very barren and rock-strewn. A small, rough track leads past it onto the heath. At 2 metres tall this was an obvious object to align upon when crossing this empty space.

The stone is of non-uniform profile and rises to a sharp point. It is also leaning at a slight angle. To the east is the group of cairns in the same townland on a small rise. To the south is Crohaun Hill, with its cluster of aerials, rises steeply and dominates the site. The location is at the southern end of the Monavullagh Mountains, which rise dramatically a few hundred metres to the north.

Whitestown East
Portal Tomb
OS Sheet 75: S 425 138

Directions: *From Kilmacthomas take the R677 north towards Carrick-on-Suir. Turn right at the second crossroads, after 9 kilometres. If you reach the junction with the R678 you have gone past the correct junction. After 1 kilometre turn right down a farm track to the farmhouse, where you can request permission to visit the tomb.*

Only the large, quartz-pebble-encrusted capstone of this monument is visible, because, like **Savagetown**, it is now incorporated into a field boundary. One end

The location of Whitestown East portal tomb.

of the capstone rests on the ground, while the other rests on a single upright – presumably a portal stone.

If the hedge was cleared from around it this tomb would resemble those at **Ballyquin** and **Ballindud**. Its location is very similar to that of **Ballyquin** as well: very near to a stream on flat ground at the base of a gentle slope.

This portal tomb was first recorded in 1911 by Revd Power:

> June 20th last I discovered on the lands of Whitestown East, close to the boundary of the latter with Croughataggart, and on the farm of Mr Geoffrey Murphy, a fine, partly ruined Cromlech. The monument is not recorded on either the one-inch or the six-inch ordnance map, though how the officers of the survey managed to overlook it, as well as others of its class, it is not easy to understand. As I have not seen the new (largest scale) ordnance sheets I do not know whether the most recent survey has recorded this prehistoric survival. The covering stone is of great size and weight – larger I think, than the covering stone of the Knockeen Cromlech; it is roughly oval in outline and measures some 15 feet in greater by about 11 feet in lesser diameter.[57]

Mini-Gazetteer – 5km N there is an ogham stone at **Ballyquin**. 7.9km NW there is a portal tomb at **Sheskin**. 11.1km ESE there is a standing stone at **Powersknock**. 12.9km SSE there is a portal tomb at **Ballynageeragh**. 13.1km N there is a portal tomb at Owning (County Kilkenny).

The Harp Stone, Whitfield North.

Whitfield North – The Harp Stone
Standing Stone
OS Sheets 75 & 76: S 540 084

Directions: *From Waterford follow the N25 west and take the first left-hand turn after the R682. Approximately 1 kilometre along this road there is an overgrown track on the right. This is very difficult to see and equally hard to park near. Walk up this track until you reach a gate. The stone is visible in the field beyond this gate.*

The short walk to this powerful-looking stone is along an overgrown farm track with high hedges on either side. This adds an air of mystery and expectation that is slightly dampened when you reach the end of the track where it opens into a wide field with power lines running across it. However, it is at this point that you first see the stone, which does take your mind off the pylons.

The towering electricity pylons create the illusion that this standing stone is much smaller than it actually is. At over 3 metres tall it starts to get very big, very quickly as you near it.

One edge is almost straight, but the other has a projection that emerges half-way up and curves outwards. This profile has given the stone its colloquial name – The Harp Stone – although when I asked a local lady for directions to the stone using this name, she had never heard it called that in the forty years she had lived in the townland.

Mini-Gazetteer – 6.2km E there is a portal tomb at **Ballindud**. 7.2km SSW there is a portal tomb at **Dunhill**. 10.8km SW there is a standing stone at **Ballingary**. 14.3km ESE there is a passage tomb at **Harristown**.

Acknowledgements

My family, especially my wife Uta, have been very supportive throughout this endeavour. Uta has, once again, read and reread the manuscript and offered corrections and comments. I have taken most of these onboard, but have ignored a few, making any mistakes my own.

I certainly could not have researched this book without the work of the archaeologists that have excavated several of the Waterford monuments and published their findings. Luckily, these sites were excavated in the times when excavation was done on a large-scale purely to investigate the monuments and learn about them. This does not happen enough; these days the vast majority of excavation work is done to 'preserve through record' before sites are destroyed and built upon.

The farmers throughout the county have been extremely generous when allowing me access to their land: this book would certainly not have been possible without them.

To all the people who have encouraged me to continue with this book after reading *Monu-Mental About Prehistoric Dublin*, I also offer my thanks.

Thank you to Nonsuch Publishing for having faith in this series and all the people there who have worked on this book to get it to press.

Notes

1) Ryland, Revd R.H., *The History, Topography and Antiquities of the County and City of Waterford; With an Account of the Present State of the Peasantry of that Part of the South of Ireland* (John Murray, 1824), p.111.

2) ibid. p.109.

3) Mark Chapman (unpublished).

4) Moore, M., *A Bronze Age Settlement and Ritual Centre in the Monavullagh Mountains, County Waterford* (Proceedings of the Prehistoric Society, 1995).

5) Budd, P. et al., *Tin Sources for Prehistoric Bronze Production in Ireland* (Antiquity no. 260, 1994).

6) Ó Nualláin and Walsh, P., *A Reconsideration of the Tramore Passage Tombs* (Proceedings of the Prehistoric Society – vol. 52, 1986).

7) Ashbee, Paul, *Ancient Scilly* (David & Charles, 1974), p.74, p.82, etc.

8) Hencken, H. O'Neill, *Cornwall and Scilly* (Methuen & Co. Ltd, 1932), p.15.

9) Wood-Martin, W.G., *Pagan Ireland: An Archaeological Sketch* (Loughmans, Green & Co., 1895), p.130.

10) 'Excavation of a Megalithic Tomb at Harristown, Co. Waterford' (JRSAI, vol. 71, pt 4, 1941).

11) Ryland, Revd R.H., *The History, Topography and Antiquities of the County and City of Waterford; With an Account of the Present State of the Peasantry of that Part of the South of Ireland* (John Murray, 1824), p.243.

12) Borlase, W.C., *Dolmens of Ireland* (Chapman & Hall, 1897), vol. I, p.63.

13) Ryland, Revd R.H., *The History, Topography and Antiquities of the County and City of Waterford; With an Account of the Present State of the Peasantry of that Part of the South of Ireland* (John Murray, 1824), p.247.

14) Powell, T.G.E., 'Excavation of a Megalithic Tomb at Carriglong, Co. Waterford' (*Journal of the Cork Historical and Archaeological Society*, vol. 46, 1941).

15) Ó Nualláin, Seán and Walsh, Paul, *A Reconstruction of the Tramore Passage-Tombs* (Proceedings of the Prehistoric Society, 1986), vol. 52, p.25.

16) Fergusson, John, *Rude Stone Monuments* (John Murray, 1872).

17) Du Noyer, George, 'On Cromleacs Near Tramore in the County of Waterford; With Remarks on the Classification of Ancient Irish Earthen and Megalithic Structures' (*Journal of the Kilkenny Archaeological Society*, 1864-66), p.479.

18) Ibid. – facing p.479.

19) Ryland, Revd R.H., *The History, Topography and Antiquities of the County and City of Waterford; With an Account of the Present State of the Peasantry of that Part of the South of Ireland* (John Murray, 1824), p.267.

20) 'The Portal Dolmens of South-Eastern Ireland' (*Journal of the Waterford Spelæological Society*, 1941).

21) *Archaeological Inventory of County Waterford* (Wordwell Press, 1999).

22) Power, Revd P., 'On a Cup-and-Circle-Inscribed Stone From County Waterford' (*Journal of the Waterford and South-East of Ireland Archaeological Society*, 1907), p.169-170.

23) Twohig, Elizabeth Shee, 'A "Problem" Solved: The Location of the Stone with Rock-Art From Mothel, County Waterford (JRSAI – vol. 127, 1997).

24) Grubb, Isabel, 'Notes on Two Prehistoric Burial Sites in the Townland of Seskin, Co. Waterford' (JRSAI – vol. 74, 1944).

25) Personal comment – local farmer.

26) Ferguson, Sir Samuel, *Ogham Inscriptions in Ireland, Scotland and Wales* (David Douglas, 1887), p.78.

27) See photo by 'Alan S' on The Modern Antiquarian website – http://www.themodernantiquarian. com/post/15862/images/boherboy.html – link valid 07-2007.

28) Powell, T.G.E., 'Excavation of a Megalithic Tomb at Ballynamona Lower, Co. Waterford' (JRSAI, vol. 68 1938).

29) Ryland, Revd R.H., *The History, Topography and Antiquities of the County and City of Waterford; With an Account of the Present State of the Peasantry of that Part of the South of Ireland* (John Murray, 1824), p.326.

30) Wood-Martin, W.G., *Pagan Ireland: An Archaeological Sketch* (Loughmans, Green & Co., 1895), p.310.

31) Ibid. p311.

32) Dowd, Marion et al., *The Human Remains from Irish Caves Project* (Archaeology Ireland – autumn 2006), p.17.

33) Twohig, Elizabeth Shee, 'A "Problem" Solved: The Location of the Stone with Rock-Art From Mothel, County Waterford (JRSAI – vol. 127, 1997).

34) Weir, Anthony, *Early Ireland: A Field Guide* (Blackstaff Press, 1980) p.122.

35) Du Noyer, George, 'On Cromleacs Near Tramore in the County of Waterford; With Remarks on the Classification of Ancient Irish Earthen and Megalithic Structures' (*Journal of the Kilkenny Archaeological Society*, 1864-66), facing p.480.

36) Herity, M., 'The Finds from the Irish Portal Dolmens' (JRSAI, vol. 94, 1964), p.135.

37) Powell, T.G.E., 'Excavation of a Megalithic Tomb at Ballynamona Lower, Co. Waterford' – T.G.E. Powell (JRSAI – vol. 68, 1938).

38) Borlase, W.C., *Dolmens of Ireland* (Chapman & Hall, vol. I, 1897), p.56.

39) *Archaeological Inventory of County Waterford* (Government of Ireland, 1999), p.197.

40) Ferguson, Sir Samuel, *Ogham Inscriptions in Ireland, Scotland and Wales* (David Douglas, 1887).

41) Taylor, Andy, *A Glimpse of Other Days* (ebook – http://snap.waterfordcoco.ie/WebRoot$/ collections/ebooks/106989/A%20glimpse%20of%20other%20%20days.pdf).

42) Powell, T.G.E., 'Excavation of a Megalithic Tomb at Carriglong, Co. Waterford' (*Journal of the Cork Historical and Archaeological Society*, vol. 46, 1941), p.55-62.

43) Ibid., p.61.

44) O'Kelly, M.J., 'A Wedge-Shaped Gallery Grave at Baurnadomeeny, Co. Tipperary' (*Journal of the Cork Historical and Archaeological Society*, vol. 65, 1960).

45) Taylor, Andy, *A Glimpse of Other Days* (ebook – http://snap.waterfordcoco.ie/WebRoot$/ collections/ebooks/106989/A%20glimpse%20of%20other%20%20days.pdf).

46) *Archaeological Inventory of County Waterford* (Government of Ireland, 1999) p.197.

47) Barry, Revd E., 'On Three Ogham Stones, Near Kilmacthomas' (*Journal of the Waterford and South-East of Ireland Archaeological Society*, vol. 2, 1896), p.228.

48) *Archaeological Inventory of County Waterford* (Government of Ireland, 1999) p.198.

49) Ibid. p.2.

50) Borlase, W.C., *Dolmens of Ireland* (Chapman & Hall, vol. 1, 1897), p.56.

51) Ryland, Revd R.H., *The History, Topography and Antiquities of the County and City of Waterford; With an Account of the Present State of the Peasantry of that Part of the South of Ireland* (John Murray, 1824), p.294.

52) Hawkes, Jaquetta, 'Excavation of a Megalithic Tomb at Harristown, Co. Waterford' (JRSAI, vol. 71, 1941).

53) Molleson, Theyla, 'New Radiocarbon Dates for the Occupation of Kilgreany Cave, County Waterford' (*Journal of Irish Archaeology*, 1985/6).

54) Dowd, Marion et al., 'The Human Remains from Irish Caves Project' (*Archaeology Ireland*, autumn 2006), p.18.

55) *Archaeological Inventory of County Waterford* (Government of Ireland, 1999), p.35.

56) Ryland, Revd R.H., *The History, Topography and Antiquities of the County and City of Waterford; With an Account of the Present State of the Peasantry of that Part of the South of Ireland* (John Murray, 1824), p.263.

57) Powell, Revd P., 'An Unrecorded Cromlech' (*Journal of the Waterford and South-East of Ireland Archaeological Society*, vol. 14, 191).